THE TRAINED KILLERS

This satirical sketch was drawn by the author on October 5, 1957, the day after Russia launched Sputnik I. It depicts the conflicting reactions of the military at that time. One officer stares in horror at Russia's technological triumph while a G.I. soldier-scientist is trying to work out the formulas needed to catch up to the enemy's technology. A second officer is restraining the Sergeant who is determined to get his hands on the G.I. who he views as malingering. The G.I., caught between these opposing expectations, is totally engrossed in his calculations and seems oblivious to the raging conflict.

Also by Joseph N. Manfredo

Only The Living
(A Memoir)

After Midnight
(Poems and Pontifications)

THE TRAINED KILLERS

Joseph N. Manfredo

Order this book online at www.trafford.com
or email orders@trafford.com

Most Trafford titles are also available at major online book retailers.

Print information available on the last page.

ISBN: 978-1-4269-7433-5 (sc)
ISBN: 978-1-4269-7434-2 (hc)
ISBN: 978-1-4269-7435-9 (e)

Library of Congress Control Number: 2011912350

Trafford rev. 10/11/2011

 www.trafford.com

North America & international
toll-free: 1 888 232 4444 (USA & Canada)
fax: 812 355 4082

To the scientists and engineers of the Scientific and
Professional Detachment
Who served their country without losing their
sense of humor.
Thanks for the memories.

Epigraph

"You gonna cost the gummint twenny thowsen dollahs ta become trained killahs! We gonna teach you a lotta ways ta kill da enemy befo' he kills you! You gonna leave here a warriah, a trained killah! Gonna come a time when you life gonna depend on it, so pay attenshun!"

Drill Sergeant, Fort Dix, New Jersey
January, 1956

PREFACE

This memoir is based on real events with slight embellishments intended to lend some color to an olive drab tapestry. It recounts what happened to an unusual group of young men during an unusual time in our military history.

After the Korean War the very real Cold War intensified between the United States and the Soviet Union. These men were drafted into the United States Amy during that period. They fought the enemy on the battlefield of science and technology in the race for domination of land, sea and space. This is not the story of that battle, but of the everyday events they experienced as they bounced between laboratory projects, routine army assignments and free time activities. It is the stuff they may never think to tell their grandchildren, yet it deserves telling.

Any similarity to actual persons or places that might get the author into trouble is purely coincidental and vigorously denied.

In the vernacular of the trade: *Some names, locations and events have been fictionalized.*

ACKNOWLEDGMENTS

A very belated thank you to the news reporters of Baltimore radio station WBAL, the Baltimore Sun newspaper and to the several United States Congressmen who worked so hard to expose and correct the misapplication of technical talents during the early years of the Cold War

My thanks, also, to companion and fellow traveler, Jo Ann St. Claire, whose critical reviews, opinions and suggestions have been so helpful in giving the book a more distaff perspective. Every author needs a Jo Ann

CONTENTS

PART I

Fort Dix

1. GREETINGS

Friday morning, 6:30 AM, 1955: The alarm went off.

I had the morning procedure carefully timed. By 6:50 I was downstairs buying a paper. At 7:05 I ordered breakfast in the Blue Belle Café across the street; orange juice, coffee, toast, two eggs – sunny side up. I climbed into my car by 7:25. It was winter in Syracuse, New York and fresh snow lay several inches deep on the streets.

The eight cylinder engine of my 1951 Pontiac roared to life despite the cold and pulled its load of vehicle and me into up-town traffic at exactly 7:30. By 7:45 the warm and growling engine purred into silence in the Salaried Personnel parking lot of the plant where I worked. I walked rapidly to the building and into my office. As I removed my jacket and gloves the large wall clock snapped to 8:00 AM. I was on time again.

It had been a good week. The money was good. Overtime was abundant due to the pressure of a new car model year. The Brown-Lipe-Chapin Division of General Motors contained steel stamping dies, forming dies, zinc die casting machines, rows and rows of buffing and polishing wheels and the largest electronic plating tanks in the world. Bumper guards, hood ornaments, wheel discs, instrument bezels, horn rings, and any other chrome accessory needed on General Motor's vehicles were manufactured here. The 1956 model chrome trim accessories had been designed long ago and were now being set up for mass production. As a newly graduated Engineer I was busy designing the machinery and methodology for the manufacture of these products.

We had been working ten hours a day, sometimes 6 days a week. Sleep was becoming a rarity. I seldom left work before 7 PM after which I went out with friends or to a girlfriend's home for dinner and company. On this Friday night I left her home late and started the 54 mile drive to Utica to visit my parents for the weekend.

I arrived well after midnight. Mom and Dad were up waiting— something they had learned not to do a long time ago. On the kitchen table lay an envelope. Mom handed it to me with a look of concern. I noted the return address and already knew what it was. It began, "Greetings." I felt a giddy sense of laxity and resignation until reading it a second time brought on a mixture of curiosity, excitement and apprehension. I was ordered to report for induction at the Syracuse induction center in one month.

The start of the Korean War caused Congress to enact a mandatory draft just as I was graduating from High School, five years earlier. At the time I was 17 years old and a prime candidate for the military on my next birthday. However, by then I was enrolled in an engineering college. As a consequence I received a "critical skills" deferment which would last until graduation.

That deferment had expired just a month ago. In accordance with the terms of the deferment I now faced two years of active military duty followed by three years of active reserve, then one year of standby reserve—a six year commitment.

The Korean War had ended in a truce. It was on hold. Both sides agreed to stop fighting, for now. There had been no winners. There had been many losers; the thousands of dead and wounded on both sides. The mandatory draft had ended but Congress had not rescinded the mandatory six year commitment of deferred students. They had, however, cancelled all educational and insurance benefits. There was no longer a GI Bill of Rights for those now being drafted.

I would serve in the armed forces of the United States during a relatively peaceful time, provided hostilities did not break out again, anywhere in the world, within the next six years. It was the early years of the strategic and technological race for supremacy between the Soviet Union and the United States which became known as the Cold War.

The following Monday morning I showed the letter to my department manager. My school buddy, fraternity brother and co-worker, Chuck Shaver, had received the same letter. We had one month to make arrangements.

The office staff threw a magnificent going away party for us with food, music and presents. Someone had put a lot of thought into that because they gave us each a suitcase set and toiletry travel kits. Chuck and I sang a duet, putting our own words to a popular song of the time, "You're Gonna Miss Me When I'm Gone." Our friends laughed. Our girlfriends cried. It was wonderful.

On the appointed day I picked Chuck up and drove to the Syracuse induction center where we were joined by a group of candidates just like us. There were several I remembered from my high school days. We joked nervously as we lined up for each stage of the induction process. One kid was sent home because his blood test showed too much sugar, the result of eating doughnuts for breakfast. He was ordered to return another day. A couple more were released for poor eyesight, bad feet or other serious physical ailments. I lost track of Chuck for a while.

After being subjected to the nefarious "short arm inspection," the old "bend and spread 'em," and the "turn your head and cough" procedures they pronounced me fit for duty. Chuck came to me and, with relief and embarrassment told me that he had been rejected. I don't recall exactly why......something to do with his eyesight or teeth or both. He wore thick eyeglasses and partial dentures.

I envied his escape from the draft. He would return to his girlfriend and his engineering job. But, on reflection, I did not envy the fact that when we went to work the next day he would have to tell everyone he had been rejected. And, what would he do with the farewell presents? I wondered.

We twelve survivors lined up, shoulder to shoulder, raised our right hand and took the oath to serve our country in the armed forces of the United States beginning that very moment. After the swearing in ceremony we received orders to be at the Syracuse train station in one week for transport to Fort Dix, New Jersey. There we would receive two months of indoctrination and basic military training. Subsequently we would be permanently transferred elsewhere.

The week flew by. I sat in the station, along with a dozen or so other young men, waiting for the train. It was mid-day. The huge station was eerily silent, occasional footsteps or whispered conversations echoing in the high ceilinged, marble columned station. More young men appeared, some alone, others with a girlfriend or parents. They sat, scattered around the station, seeking privacy with loved ones. Shortly several Non Commissioned Officers (NCOs) appeared wearing army uniforms. All eyes drifted in their direction. As they called out names from a clipboard the inductees, one by one, arose and answered "Here" as we had been directed. We followed the NCOs to one of the outside platforms and awaited the train's arrival.

Presently it came. As it chuffed, clanked and hissed to a stop anxious, excited voices made vapor puffs in the frigid January air. Amid the damp clouds of engine steam the recruits made their way aboard. The NCOs urged stragglers, some engaged in tearful goodbyes, to get aboard. The NCOs seemed friendly enough. They climbed aboard, told us to find a bunk for the night, and then disappeared. We were left to our own devices as the train moved out.

The atmosphere was one of jovial excitement. The unsuspecting recruits, all wearing casual civilian clothes, were in a party mood. They joked and laughed as they scrambled to lay claim to one of the Pullman bunks that lined both sides of the cars, then settled down to play cards and generally have a good time on this free train ride to New Jersey.

The train clattered on, stopping frequently at other stations where additional passengers and recruits came aboard and the noise increased with renewed intensity. I climbed into my bunk around 10 PM but it took a long time to fall asleep because of the noisy celebrants around me who remained up most of the night.

2. INDOCTRINATION

It seemed I had been asleep only a few minutes when the quiet predawn silence was broken by harsh voices bellowing into our ears. The first words I recognized were "Fall out! Fall out! Get dressed, c'mon, let's go!!" There was general bewilderment. No one, it seemed, had anticipated this rude, early morning awakening. I looked out the window. It was still dark outside. I squinted at my watch. It was only 5 AM. They couldn't be serious, could they? They were.

Guys who had trouble awakening were told, "You're in the Army now! This ain't your Mama's house. Get up and get dressed! Let's go! Move it!"

A few of the slower witted guys complained and received immediate, personal, unwanted attention. Most of us learned quickly to overcome our shock and outrage. From that moment on we were told what to do, when to do it and how to do it.

The train stopped one final time and we filed off, mostly subdued, sleepy, tired and confused. We filed onto buses and tried to catch a few more winks as they threaded through the countryside. They came to a stop at a guard house manned by several Military Police dressed in sharply creased uniforms, wearing white gloves. After formalities the bus entered and drove another mile or so. It pulled over and we filed out onto a blacktop area. I looked around at the sterile buildings, the uniformed soldiers and the marching platoons

7

of men keeping cadence to the drone of drill sergeants, "Hut, Hoo, Haree, Hore.......Hut.......Hut!"

This was Fort Dix, New Jersey.

We were introduced to the "hurry and wait" syndrome of the United States Army. After being rushed from the buses and jogging across an open area we stood in a long line at the entrance of a large warehouse. Here we received our Government Issue (GI) army clothes, boots, dog tags, shoeshine gear, helmet liner, helmet and a twenty dollar bill, our first pay. It was dubbed the "flying twenty" because we were immediately charged for some of the things issued to us and, poof, it was gone.

We moved into another room where we changed out of our civilian clothing and into the GI clothing. With our "civvies" rolled up under one arm we lined up outdoors. We were strongly encouraged to donate our discarded civilian clothing to a local charitable organization. It might have been the Salvation Army. I dumped every civilian stitch I had—shoes, socks, underwear, shirt, pants and jacket—on a large heap on the ground at the foot of a sign bearing the name of said charity. For the next 60 days everything I wore was olive drab, khaki or brown.

I already knew my Selective Service Number, a nine digit number. I now memorized my United States Army Serial Number—US followed by 8 more digits. Every article of clothing was stamped with the initial of my last name and the last four digits of my serial number—M0767. That became part of my new identification.

Training started immediately. We fell out, shoulder to shoulder, for the first time, dressed in our new army fatigues and boots. Here we would be subjected to the hazing intended to demolish and eradicate all our prior years of life experience.

"I am your drill Sergeant! I am your Mother! I am your Father! I am your brother, your sister, your aunt and your uncle! Forget your girlfriend! You belong to me! You will do exactly as you are told! You will not call me Sir! You will call me Sergeant! If I ask you a question you will answer it 'Yes, Sergeant' or 'No, Sergeant'! I will tell you when to come and when to go, when to wake and when to sleep, when to eat and when to s—t!"

Ideas of individuality would be wiped out and our minds reduced to clean slates, devoid of old concepts, ready for a new set of rules and regulations.

This was brought home powerfully as we were lined up outside the barber shop where, within two minutes, to the angry buzz of electric clippers, our carefully nurtured curls and waves, heavy sideburns and ducktail styles floated to the floor. Our heads were reduced to shiny-skinned skulls.

These new experiences were intended to imbue a sense of blind obedience to military authority. Concurrently, our physical conditioning would begin and we would learn all the basic skills of how to kill another human being. We would leave Fort Dix, we were told, as trained killers at a cost to the United States taxpayers of $20,000 each, a lot of money in 1956.

Our first housing was a set of single story barracks, each accommodating around 20 recruits on side by side bunks. A resident Corporal slept in a private room in one corner of each barrack. His principle duty, it appeared, was to use intimidation, harassment and abuse to teach us how to rise before dawn, make a bed, shower, shave, shine boots, dress in battle fatigues and generally learn the regimented life style of military life. This consisted mostly of standing in line and waiting.

Our barrack's Corporal, a man with a deep southern drawl, was especially fond of yelling directly into your face whenever he spoke to you. His tall, muscular frame leaned forward from the waist so he could push his face into yours while shouting.

His favorite pastime was to inspect our freshly made beds for "alligators," small wrinkles that escaped our notice, or square corners that had even a trace of wrinkle in the blanket. When he found one, he tore the bed apart and threw the blanket, sheets, pillow and mattress out the nearest open window into the snow bank outside. We retrieved them and again made the bed. This procedure was repeated a number of times. He screamed, cursed, threatened us with mayhem then threw the bedding out the window due to real or imaginary "alligators," as the spirit moved him. That first morning he tore apart and threw out the window the blankets, sheets, pillows, and mattresses of every single bunk at least three times. Eventually he declared them, one by one, to be satisfactory.

Ah, but then he made the rounds with a 25 cent piece. He bounced the quarter on each finished bed. If it failed to bounce high enough to please him he again tore the bed apart and threw it out the window. Once in a while, if he felt like it, and to demonstrate his absolute power over us, he ordered us to run, in our underwear, around the outside of the barracks, in the deep, cold New Jersey snow, until he felt we were properly chastised and humbled. Our initial outrage at these injustices—slowly for some, rapidly for others—turned to acceptance of the fact that he did have absolute power that must be obeyed without rationale and without hesitation. We were learning.

This Corporal occasionally picked out a recruit and ordered him into his private room. He closed the door, sometimes for a few minutes, sometimes for an hour or so. When the door opened and the recruit came out we stared in silent wonder about what had happened. If asked the recruits answered that he just talked to them. One recruit I had befriended told me the Corporal made small talk that eventually turned to girls and sex. I was called in just once. The Corporal had little to say. He sat quietly for a long time fussing with something at his desk, then asked if I had a girlfriend. I said I did. He sent me out. One shy young fellow, who was in there longer than usual, was called in several more times over the next few days. He never spoke to us about what went on. When asked he would respond, "Nothing."

After a week we were transferred to other barracks in a different part of the base where more intense combat training would commence. The day before we moved out our Corporal was replaced. We were told he was facing demotion for making us run in the snow in our underwear. Unofficial scuttlebutt was that he had been sexually abusing one or more of the timid recruits.

3. Furnace Duty

Our new barracks were located some distance further into the base. There were no cadre living in the barracks, just raw recruits. We had several drill sergeants who lived in their own barracks or off base and drove in each morning. They reported to Master Sergeant Ciecca, a seasoned older man who was tough as nails. His gruff, crusty exterior was menacing. A veteran of World War II and Korea, Master Sergeant Ciecca was spending the remainder of his career training new recruits. He had overseen the training of countless young men who served in the Korean conflict. His power extended over our entire company. His lesser sergeants were younger but equally tough and demanding. Their job was to condition us and prepare us for combat.

On our first day of training we were given a class on how to stoke, bank and care for a coal furnace, just like the ones in the furnace room of each barrack. We took a test to see how much we had learned. As a recent college graduate I had a deeply ingrained habit of trying to do my very best on any test, striving for a perfect score. I had been doing so for the past dozen years. I gave it my best shot and was proud that I was one of six men who got perfect scores on the test. They congratulated us and told us we now belonged to the furnace maintenance team. We were the company firemen. I wondered what that entailed. We soon found out.

While others slept at night we took turns stoking the furnaces in the barracks all night long. At the crack of dawn we were expected to change, shower, shave, dress and fall out for roll call along with all the others, regardless of the fact that we had had little or no sleep all night.

After several weeks of being exhausted from hard days of training and long nights of shoveling coal and ashes I developed a horrible, itching skin rash on my upper torso. It was the exact shape of my 100% wool GI undershirt. I couldn't sleep even during the nights I was not on furnace duty. I went on sick call. The Doctors were not sure what it was. They said it happened often to new recruits. No one knew what caused it and there was no cure. They gave me a bottle of Calamine lotion and some cotton balls. When I applied it I felt relief for all of about 20 minutes. On nights when I did not have furnace duty I lay awake feeling like caterpillars were crawling on my skin.

Years of training as a conscientious civilian kept me from letting the fires die. Then I noticed that the less dependable guys, who let the furnace fires die, were relieved from the roster and I was picking up their nights, too. I grit my moral and ethical teeth.

The first time was the toughest. I let one furnace go out as I sneaked a nap in the furnace room. The next night I killed a couple more fires and took a longer nap. I endured curses and humiliation from several sergeants and some of the recruits. But I was getting more sleep. The third night all the furnaces went out as I spent the whole night cuddled in a furnace room. Everyone awoke to cold showers and freezing barracks. I was removed from the fireman roster. We had to shower, wash and shave in cold water. I slept more hours every night and the rash went away as mysteriously as it had appeared.

That was the last time I tried to appear bright in the army. From that day forward I avoided the appearance that I could even tie my shoes correctly.

I had learned the wise recruit's mantra: "Keep a low profile and never volunteer for anything!"

4. Things We Learned

We learned many things the hard way.

We learned early on that if we didn't shave every day before Reveille we'd be forced to shave with a dry razor—no cream, no soap, no water, outdoors, in the predawn darkness, in full view of the platoon for maximum lesson by example.

We learned to read the company bulletin board before going to bed to see what we were supposed to wear the next morning—the Uniform of The Day—and not to deviate from that instruction.

One night, like most, the Uniform of the Day read combat fatigues, boots, field jacket and helmet liner. The next morning, the troop awoke to a heavy rain storm. They put on the Uniform of the Day, then, as their Mothers had taught them, donned rain ponchos before going out into the rain. They fell into formation and stood at attention.

The Sergeant walked slowly up and down the front rank. He stopped in front of one recruit, put his face into the soldiers face and asked, in a kindly, fatherly voice, "What was the Uniform of the Day, Smith?"

"Combat fatigues, boots, field jacket, helmet liner, Sergeant!"

The Sergeant tilted his head sideways to signify puzzlement. "Then why are you wearing a poncho, Smith?"

"It's raining, Sergeant."

"No. See, that is a weather report, Smith. I did not ask for a weather report, Smith. I'm wondering why you are wearing a poncho, Smith."

"Well, uh, I'd get wet without it, Sergeant."

"Did the Uniform of the Day bulletin say if it is raining and you don't want to get wet you should wear a poncho, Smith?"

"No, Sergeant."

The Sergeant leaned back, took a deep breath and, in a voice that could be heard half way across the base, bellowed "Then take that damn poncho back to your locker and come out here in the Uniform of the Day, Smith! All the rest of you idiots who can't read, get rid of those damn ponchos! You got two minutes to get back here! Fall out! Move it!"

We ran in, put away the ponchos, ran outside and fell in. We stood there, at attention, for a full two minutes in pouring rain while he slowly walked back and forth inspecting the uniforms, the freshly shaven faces.

Then he said, "Company! I have observed that it is raining. You may get wet without your rain gear. You are to fall out, put on ponchos and fall in! You've got two minutes! Fall out!"

We ran inside, put on ponchos, ran outside, fell in and stood at attention. We stood in the rain wearing ponchos over wet fatigues while the Sergeant casually took roll call. The rubberized ponchos trapped the moisture inside. After a while we were cold, clammy and miserable. The lesson learned: do not think for yourselves!

We were introduced to our rifles. Holding one above his head the Sarge intoned:

"This is the M-1 Garand 30-06 caliber, gas operated, semi-automatic, clip-fed rifle. It weighs 9 ½ pounds without ammo and is 43.6 inches long. When the last round fires the clip is automatically ejected and the bolt locks open, ready for another clip. A skilled soldier can get off 40 to 50 accurate shots in a minute and be effective at a range of 300 yards. This is your new girlfriend. Just like your old girlfriend, she will take good care of you if you take good care of her. You will not refer to her as your girlfriend. You will refer to her as your rifle. She is called a rifle because her barrel is rifled. She has helical grooves machined inside her barrel. The grooves cause your bullet to spin. That makes you, and your bullet, more accurate. She is not a gun! A gun barrel is just a smooth tube. There are no rifle grooves inside a gun barrel. Your new girlfriend does not like to be called a gun. She will be unhappy. So will I. You do not want her, or me, to be unhappy!"

Recruits who called their rifle a gun within hearing of an NCO made that mistake only one time. They stood before the platoon, held the rifle at arm's length with one hand, gripped their crotch with the other hand and recited, loudly, "This is my rifle (shake rifle), this is my gun (shake crotch), this is for killing (shake rifle), this is for fun (shake crotch)!" Do that ten times and you will remember which is which.

We met the gas mask. This rubberized, google-eyed, multi-strapped monstrosity had a can of charcoal and some other stuff hanging from the end of an elephant's trunk. The only thing that could motivate you to put one of these things on was the threat of a painful, horrible death if you didn't. The lecture was delivered while we sat on bleachers in an open field. The NCO described what certain gases smelled like so that, in the event of gas warfare, we might recognize and identify what type of gas was about to kill us and how it would kill us. Phosgene, for example, smelled like the Hawthorne bush or new mown hay. When combined with the moisture in your eyes or lungs it decomposes into hydrochloric acid which leads to burning, nausea, vomiting and headaches. In 4 to 72 hours it could lead to pulmonary edema, pneumonia and cardiac problems. Nerve gas, on the other hand, did even more awful things and did them quickly. It had no odor. The mask probably was of no use for nerve gas but gave a false sense of security.

The graphic descriptions of what these gases could do to us served as powerful motivators to learn all about how to use gas masks.

"If you smell gas you better shout 'Gas!' then put on your mask and clear it before you try to help some other poor slob! If you hear somebody shout 'Gas!' you better do the same thing, only faster."

To see if we had been paying attention an instructor, hiding beneath the bleachers and wearing a gas mask, discharged a tear gas canister. As it floated up to us the lead instructor grinned and watched as we sat stupidly for precious seconds. They were delighted as we fumbled with our masks, coughing and gasping.

There was only one way, they said, to be sure that it was safe to remove our masks. There would be no test kits. There was no clever method to check for safe, clear air.

"You're gonna ask for a volunteer to remove his mask and test the air. If nobody volunteers you all are going to pick out the least useful man in your troop and forcefully remove his mask. He might struggle so get a good grip and watch him breathe. If he suffers or dies, clearly ya better wait a while longer."

We were also warned that if our chosen 'volunteer' lived he might not be in a pleasant frame of mind after this and should be watched closely.

Our last gas training exercise took place in a one room building designed for this purpose. We waited in line outside the building and received instructions. The building was filled with tear gas. Two Sergeants were inside, wearing gas masks. We were to enter, one at a time, holding our breath, with our masks still snapped in their holders at our hips. We were to then pull out the mask, place it over our face, strap it over our head, clear it, and start breathing. We must stand and wait until a Sergeant signaled us to leave through the back door. Once outside the masks could be removed. If it was done properly we would experience some mild discomfort. If a recruit panicked inside the building things could go wrong in a hurry.

Percival Pugh was our biggest worry. He was a short kid, with two unnaturally long, very bushy, arched eyebrows that almost met in the middle, over close-set little eyes. He wore oversized, black-rimmed glasses. His eyelids were always half closed as if he had taken a sleeping pill. His ears were too large for his small face. He breathed through his mouth and had almost no chin at all. His uniform was always disheveled and baggy on him. He often forgot to button his shirt and sometimes tripped over loose boot laces.

16

Percy never could seem to get things straight. He recently gave out cigars to some of us because his girlfriend wrote telling him she was pregnant and he might be the father. She wasn't sure. He was so proud that it might be him.

A few days earlier our platoon was walking, side by side, through a field combat drill, firing our rifles from the hip at pop-up targets. Percy kept dropping behind me and firing past my ear. Each time I heard the snap of the bullet passing me I flinched, turned and swore at him. Finally I dragged him forward by his shirt front and said I would shoot him the next time he dropped behind me. He trotted, stiff-legged, one yard ahead of me after that, looking back over his shoulder with justifiable fear and firing erratically at no particular target.

At the tear gas house Percy hung back, waiting to be the last because he was afraid. The entire platoon had gone through the tear gas house and was waiting outside the back door for Percy to appear. Finally the door burst open and out he flew, head first, propelled by a leg and a large boot that had just kicked him in the ass. Gagging and puking, Percy dropped to the ground, his mask still clutched tightly in his hand, tears, vomit and spittle dripping from eyes, nose and mouth.

We looked at each other and reached an unspoken, unanimous decision. Nods of agreement were exchanged. In the event our platoon ever suffered a real gas attack we would test for clear air by removing Percival Pugh's gas mask.

5. THE TARGET RANGE

Company 2, consisting of 56 recruits, made a number of trips to the shooting range. We spent three days there practicing rifle and machine gun fire. On the last several days we were tested and rated for our skill level at various distances from the targets. Perfect scores won Expert medals. Acceptable scores won Sharpshooter medals, and so on down to no medal.

A deep trench was located at the farthest end of the field. In this trench other soldiers worked the ropes and pulleys that raised and lowered bull's eye targets. At 50 yard intervals firing lines were marked by long, white chalk lines on the ground. Each firing line was marked with individual firing positions so that each position was clearly lined up with one of the targets. Recruits lie in a prone position and followed instructions on when and how to fire at the targets. After each exercise soldiers in the target trench raised a round red disk on the end of a pole and held it for a few seconds over each bullet hole so the recruit could see how he had done. If a recruit missed the target with one or more of his three shots the man in the trench waved a red flag for each missed shot. After completing a couple practice sets of three rounds each we had a final test set and were scored for accuracy. Then we moved back another 50 yards to the next firing line and repeated the process.

Several short, white posts were located along each firing line. They held phone jacks. The Lieutenant used one of these to plug in his portable phone so he could communicate with the control tower which was behind the farthest firing line and centered on the rows. The Lieutenant wore a shiny white helmet with Lieutenant bars painted on it so the tower could distinguish him from the rest of us. The rest of us wore an olive drab steel helmet which we affectionately called a "pot."

At each firing line two Sergeants gave us orders, one on the left half of the line, another on the right half. They ordered us to assume a prone position with our rifles. Sergeants passed out one loaded clip of ammunition to each recruit, usually only three rounds, to establish a shot pattern.

They instructed us to load the clips. We shoved the clip in through the breech. When the Sergeants were satisfied they signaled to our Lieutenant. He used his phone to tell the tower we were ready. The tower then spoke over a public address system and this procedure followed:

"Lock and load one round Ball ammunition," the tower instructed.

Recruits pulled back the bolt and let it slam forward, inserting a live round into the firing chamber. The remaining rounds would automatically enter the breech after each shot.

"Ready on the right?"

A Sergeant gave an OK signal.

"Ready on the left?"

The other Sergeant also signaled.

"Ready on the firing line!" the tower declared.

"Targets up!" came the voice from the tower.

Soldiers in the trench hoisted fresh targets above their heads.

"Commence Fire!"

And the shooting began until all clips were exhausted. Long, sporadic, ragged reports, were accompanied by the light metallic clinks of empty clips being ejected. There was always one very late shot. Silence fell.

"Cease fire! Cease fire!" came from the tower.

By our second day at the target range we knew what to expect from the cadre. The Sergeants, who were older men, were tough, but reasonable, intent that we should become proficient and earn those medals. The Second Lieutenant, a very young man, was a different story. Lacking in actual experience he depended on bullying and sarcasm to motivate the recruits. When a soldier's shot pattern was off a Sergeant came over and offered advice, crudely but helpfully. Our Lieutenant shouted obscenities and ridicule. When a red flag waved, signifying a miss, the Lieutenant stood over the hapless soldier and ranted until he felt the man was sufficiently humiliated.

That morning we had completed firing from the 100 yard line and had just moved back to the 150 yard line.

"Firing positions!" shouted our Sergeants. We went to the ground and accepted the clips. We loaded the clips. One last inspection by the Sergeants, then signals were made to the tower. The tower spoke.

"Lock and load one round Ball ammunition!"

56 bolts slammed a live round home. Each rifle held three live rounds. 168 live rounds were about to be unleashed on the targets.

Our Lieutenant suddenly began running back and forth behind us shouting, "Watch out for the white helmet! If any of you bastards hit that white helmet I'll have your ass! Don't hit that helmet!"

I looked for it and there it was, sitting on one of the short, white telephone jack poles at the 100 yard line. The Lieutenant had placed it there during the last exercise and forgotten to put it back on his head when we moved back to 150 yards. We had not noticed it until he brought it to our attention.

"Ready on the right?" asked the tower.

"Don't hit it! I'm warning you!"

"Ready on the left?" queried the tower.

"I'm warning you! I'll have your ass!"

"Ready on the firing line!" shouted the tower.

"If you miss your target I'll know it was you!!"

"Targets up!"

56 sets of eyes began sighting on bull's eye targets. Recruits remembered their training; "Don't jerk on the trigger. Gently squeeze it like it was your girlfriend's breast." 56 nervous index fingers tightened, slowly and softly on triggers.

"Commence Fire!"

A shot rang out. The helmet spun around. More shots followed. The helmet danced, then flew off the post. It flipped in the air and fell to the ground where it jigged and bounced amidst bursts of sand and dirt until the sound of the last shot faded.

"Cease fire! Cease fire!" commanded the tower.

"Son of a bitch! Son of a bitch! The bastard who missed his target is gonna be court martialed! That helmet cost forty bucks! You'll pay for it, too! Son of a bitch!" the Lieutenant screamed as he pranced and paced back and forth behind us.

He fell silent as a red flag on the end of a pole slowly came up from the target trench and waved left and right in front of one target. His eyes lit up and he grinned.

"AHA!" he shouted, "I've gottcha, you bastard!" He started walking rapidly to the shooter who was lying in line with that target.

Another red flag rose up and started slowly waving. The Lieutenant stopped and looked back at the other soldier. He reversed direction, unsure which soldier to approach first. Then a third red flag came up, and a fourth and another and another until 56 targets had red flags waving slowly back and forth.

That day 56 riflemen had failed to pass the 150 yard test on that first set. But they scored 56 nicely grouped bullet patterns on the second 150 yard set, later that same day.

Go figure.

6. Marches and Charges

I discovered early in basic training that new recruits from New York City were regarded by the cadre as smart alecs and trouble makers. When asked where I was from I always specified, with careful enunciation, "Upstate New York." The cadre understood this to mean I was from somewhere else in the State of New York far from that breeding ground of wise guys, New York City.

We had a couple of superbly fit boys in our platoon who were from New York City. Because they were from "New Yawk" they, like all New Yorkers, had been subjected to harsher than usual treatment by the cadre. But, they earned the respect of the cadre during forced marches.

Our longest forced march—a timed 10 miles, with full 40 pound packs, 9½ pound rifles, bayonets, steel helmets, gas masks and full water canteens on our hips—was a severe test of physical fitness. The platoons were competing against each other. No platoon wanted to earn the title of being the poorest performing in the company. So everyone pushed themselves, sometimes resulting in short vomiting sessions by the side of the road.

The Sergeants alternated our pace, walking rapidly—quick march—with a 30 inch stride for ten minutes, then running—double time—for five minutes. With each passing mile the platoon became more strung out. A few boys began to falter and stop. Our two "New Yawkahs" came to the rescue. They had been semiprofessional boxers in the big apple and had incredible endurance. Deep into the ordeal they began dropping behind to help stragglers in our platoon. They took rifles from the stragglers to ease their load. Then, while carrying extra rifles, each pulled a straggler by the arm, almost carrying them to the head of the column. Leaving them there, they ran back to get two more. While I, and most others, struggled to get ourselves and our gear to the finish line these tremendous athletes had run the course at least twice by going back and forth on their errands of mercy. Near the end when soldiers were ready to quit they'd be urged on by our Sergeants and the rest of the platoon. One exhausted young man, unwilling to let his platoon down, began vomiting as he ran, barfing in cadence with his footfalls; urp, thump, urp, thump, urp, thump.

We knew Percival Pugh would not complete the march. He was trailing right from the start and was prepared to drop out after the first two miles. Early on our two athletes took turns carrying his rifle, his pack and dragging him, stumbling and gasping, for several miles until his legs collapsed and he became dead weight. They left him there, by the side of the road with his equipment. He cost us one demerit in the scoring. A trailing truck picked him up along with others from other platoons.

At the completion of the march we stowed our gear and reported to the mess hall for lunch. The next morning the results were posted on the company bulletin board. Despite Percy we had come in first in the company, thanks primarily to the two superhuman New Yawkahs! They were our heroes.

A frequent drill was learning the proper way to drop to the ground, whether walking or running, and fire from a prone position. When given the order to "drop and fire" we dropped, all in one motion, first to one knee, rolled forward, broke the fall with the right elbow and the rifle butt, tucked the left or forward elbow under the rifle barrel, pressed the stock into the shoulder, aimed and squeezed the trigger. This was practiced until we could do so in one, rapid, unbroken, smooth movement that took us from an upright position to a prone firing position in little more than a second or two.

We were urged to scream or yell fiercely, preferably shouting, "Kill! Kill! Kill!"—or some other equally intimidating invective—when making a charge. When a whole platoon did so, dropping and firing or plunging bayonets into straw dummies, it made a blood curdling sound.

One day, as I charged alongside my buddies, all screaming and yelling at the top of their lungs, I thought I heard a kitten mewing. I ran at the dummy hanging from one of the scaffolds, and executed the bayonet attack we had been taught. I struck the dummy under the chin with an uppercut from the rifle butt, hit it in the face with the blunt end of the butt, slashed down and to the right diagonally across its neck and chest with the cutting edge of the bayonet, then plunged the bayonet point deep into its stomach area. I placed a boot on the dummy's stomach, shoved it away and pulled the bayonet out, then resumed the charge toward the next target. Running at full speed toward the next set of dummies, my ears ringing from the killer shouts around me, I thought I heard it again, off to my left and slightly behind me. A kitten was mewing.

I turned my head slightly and glanced rearward over my shoulder. There was Ralph Madden, a malicious grin on his face, mewing for all the world like a frightened kitten.

Ralph was a tall, gentle giant of a guy who had recently graduated from law school, cum laude. It was difficult to maintain a killer's demeanor with a timid kitten mewing in my ear.

I made it a point, during any subsequent exercises like this, to be standing close to Ralph so I could hear the kitten and be reminded that this was still all make believe.

7. Cleanliness

Cleanliness is next to Godliness. Most of us were told that from early childhood. The Army told us the same thing. To enforce that we spent many hours spit shining combat boots, polishing brass and cleaning rifles. While boots and brass were important the rifle was our sacrosanct possession. Many mornings we suffered close examination, but one day we were warned by Master Sergeant Ciecca, that inspection would be especially rigorous. We were ordered to clean our rifles, polish our boots and brass then fall out for individual close inspection.

Our first rejections were for lack of reflection in our boot polish or small defects in the brass, then dirt in or on our rifles. We went back to our barracks after each rejection and corrected the mistakes, then returned to the inspection line. The rifle was dismantled into pieces and each piece inspected separately. The rifle barrel was inspected last each time by holding it up to the light and looking for anything other than a shiny, oiled cylinder. Rifle patches, small square patches of cotton cloth, were used to swab out the barrel as a last operation. These often left very tiny pieces of lint, barely visible to the naked eye. This was cause for rejection.

Back to the barracks and another swabbing out, then, back to the inspection line. This process, begun around 6 AM, went on all day long. Some of the rejections were for imaginary pieces of lint, some were clearly the inspectors resentment of a recruit's attitude or facial expression.

Eventually we all learned to go back to the barracks, without question, and swab the rifle barrel again. Timing was everything now. If we took too long between inspections the inspector would punish us for stalling. If we returned too soon the inspector would assume we had not been thorough and reject the rifle on principle. The final rifle approval came just before dinner. We were allowed to return these to the rifle rack for storage. Boots and brass cleaning, rejection and re-cleaning continued.

Eventually the brass passed. We stored them safely in our foot lockers and returned for further inspection of boots. Finally everyone passed boot inspection. We stored them safely away, too.

We gingerly placed all these sparkling clean things in their proper place. Just before bedtime we went outside to read the Uniform of the Day for the following day. The order read, "Inspection condition brass, freshly laundered combat fatigues, field jackets, helmet liners, helmets, boots, rifles." All of our just cleaned, shiny, spotless garb and weapons would be on us in the morning. This must be a final inspection, we thought. Maybe a parade of some sort!

Before dawn the next day we fell out for Reveille, all showered, shaved and dressed properly. We made a dazzling scene, neatly lined up with our spare set of freshly laundered fatigues, glistening brass and boots and pristine rifles, helmet liner and steel helmets bright in the morning sun.

Everyone passed in review and boarded waiting buses. The buses rode out to a distant field where the company disembarked and stood in platoon formation. We marched to the edge of a large field, a little larger than a football field. There we lined up shoulder to shoulder, by squad, halted and awaited instructions.

Finally a Sergeant stood before us and said that, on his command, we were to charge across that field, with rifles at the ready. Upon his second command we were to drop to the ground, roll to a prone position, aim and mock fire. It was then that we noticed the field had been flooded overnight and was now a gooey, sloppy mess of six inch deep slimy mud.

The troops were shocked. We were immaculate. Our boots sparkled. Our brass shone. Our fatigues were freshly starched and creased from the laundry. Our helmets were spotless. And our rifles, our pristine, beautiful, shiny, oily clean rifle barrels, polished stocks, spotless breeches, had never been so lovely. From early childhood most of us had learned that we should not get dirty when we were dressed nicely. This flew in the face of all that was holy.

The order for the first squad to charge came too soon. They broke raggedly, some stepping gingerly into the mud as if it were dog poop. The screams of rage from the sergeants moved them forward at a hesitant pace. Then the command, "drop and fire!" It was horrible. Men lowered themselves gingerly to the ground. Others stared stupidly down at the goop and froze. These men were given swift boot kicks in the behind and unceremoniously pitched face first into the mud. The squad was ordered to charge forward again. They stood up and did so only to be ordered to "drop and fire!" again. This continued the length of the field. Once across the field the next rank was ordered forward. Each squad went through the same gut wrenching agony, torn between years of maternal training and the terror of disobeying a direct order. Once all the squads had crossed over we began again, charging this time back across the quagmire, dropping as ordered. By the fourth crossing we were executing the charge and drop without hesitation.

Afterward we stood at attention, in formation, clothes caked with mud, wet clear through and clinging to our bodies. Our hands and faces were splattered with globs of mud. Rifles, those virginally pure rifles, were smeared with muddy water.

We had overcome years of civilian training and found we could obey a seemingly insane command, without hesitation. We could get our clean clothes and shiny boots filthy dirty and it no longer bothered us. Some of the men were smiling. Playing in the mud could be fun.

From that time on staying clean in a live combat situation was not top priority. Staying alive was.

8. Bivouac

We loaded up our gear, a 40 lb. backpack, mess kit, canteen full of water, gas mask, nine and one half pound M1A1 rifle, spare socks, and half a pup tent. Trucks took us into the countryside, a wooded area somewhere on base, presumably still in Fort Dix, New Jersey. We chose a buddy and assembled the two man pup tents on the snow dusted ground.

During that first night the snow began to fall. At morning Reveille we woke in darkness. The tents were buried under fresh snow. We dug out of the little tents by pushing open the flaps, then tunneling out.

That day we marched through the woods to an area with scattered trees. We were instructed on the proper way to dig a fox hole. Paired up with our tent buddies and, using our little trenching tools, we dug a fox hole six feet long, five feet wide and six feet deep. The sergeants inspected our fox holes to make sure we met all dimensions and had left a short step along the bottom of the walls so we could stand up and fire over the edge. In one corner of the floor we dug an angled tunnel about eight inches in diameter and a couple feet deep with a dog-leg bend near the bottom. This hole was where we were supposed to toss or kick an enemy hand grenade, if we didn't have time to toss it back out, and hope for the best. Of course, they allowed, we always had the option of throwing ourselves on the grenade to save our buddies.

31

Digging the fox hole took more than half the day. As soon as each fox hole passed inspection we were told to fill it in—another lesson in blindly obeying orders that defied logic.

Food was better during bivouac than at any other time. Trucks delivered all the equipment necessary to set up field kitchens. We had steak at almost every meal. Our steel serving trays, stacked at the head of the serving line, were cold as death. As the steaming food and sizzling steaks were dropped on our cold steel trays they congealed instantly, white grease appearing on and around steak, veggies, and plaster-hard mashed potatoes. Only the coffee and cocoa remained hot for a while.

Ralph Madden, my cum laude lawyer friend, sitting next to me, pulled his steak off the tray with his fingers and, holding it like a piece of pizza, tore chunks off with his teeth, never setting it back down on the ice cold tray. In this manner the steak retained its heat a little longer. Then he hacked into the partially frozen mashed potatoes and veggies. Long after bivouac Ralph continued eating his steak like pizza. In the warmth of the mess hall, back at camp, Ralph picked up his steak and, holding it in his finger tips, ate it a bite at a time. "I like it that way," he explained, "because it flies in the face of the inhuman regimentation of the military." He enjoyed being different.

Near our bivouac area was a depressed field used to train troops to crawl long distances under barbed wire and live machine gun fire while maneuvering around ground installed explosives to simulate live fire combat. The procedure was simple. We crouched in a trench at the far end of the field. Directly in front of us, at the opposite end, were several machine guns firing live bullets with tracers in every third round so we could see them passing overhead. On command we crawled out of the trenches and began a belly crawl, rifle cradled in the crook of our arms before us as we scrabbled forward with elbows and wiggling legs, flat on our bellies, hugging the ground. Inches above our heads the snap of passing bullets sounded like a bull whip being cracked near our helmets. An occasional ricochet whined away far behind us. If we felt or saw a small, round chicken wire fence we crawled around and away from it because it contained an explosive charge that could go off at any second to simulate incoming artillery or mortar fire. Hearts pounding, our breath ragged from exertion, we slithered the length of the field, and slid over the edge of another trench at the base of the embankment beneath the machine guns.

We did this once in the morning, without the gunfire and explosives. As we reached the safe end of the field we ran to the mess trucks where lunch was being served. We had to remove our backpacks and equipment in a designated area, open the packs, dig out our knife, fork and spoon, then run to the chow line.

The same exercise was repeated in the afternoon with live fire and explosives. After supper, in the dark, we repeated the trek, this time unable to see how far we had come or had to go, feeling with our fingers for the chicken wire explosive pits. There was no moon. The stars were hidden by low lying clouds. Tracers drew long red streaks overhead. It was much more unnerving in the dark. We could hear others but could see no one. We knew we had reached the end when we felt the edge of the far trench.

I had decided that if I hid my knife, fork and spoon in my shirt pocket before the exercise I could be among the first in the chow line. I could drop my pack and rifle and run straight to the chow line while everyone else was digging out their flatware. It worked at lunch. At supper, as I reached the chow line, I felt in my shirt pocket only to find it full of New Jersey dirt and one spoon. My knife and fork lay out there, somewhere under the machine gun fire, lost in thousands of square yards of dirt and frost. I ate with my fingers and a spoon during the rest of our time out on bivouac.

At the end of basic training, as I was being mustered out of Fort Dix I came up short one knife and one fork. My next monthly pay check was reduced by the cost of a replacement set of flatware.

9. STRANGE ROOMMATES

Two or three Cuban soldiers were housed in each barrack. They, too, were being trained for combat. They spoke no English and kept to themselves. While they attended a few of our exercises, for the most part we did not see them during the day. Perhaps they were being trained to support Cuban dictator Batista against the young revolutionary, a man named Fidel Castro. More likely they were being trained to help Castro overthrow Batista. At that time Castro was pretending, to the face of the world, to be a supporter of the United States. He openly denied to the U.S. media any Communist leanings during those early years

Of their many peculiarities the most striking behavior of the two Cubans in our barrack was that they would, whenever the urge overcame them, openly masturbate while sitting on the barrack floor, using our rifle cleaning patches to clean themselves afterwards. It was like watching animals in a zoo. They suffered no embarrassment or shame.

Among our platoon were several other recruits who behaved oddly. One poor fellow, Horace Tillman, spent all his time shining his shoes. He wandered through each day seemingly in a fog, doing everything as if in a drugged state, reacting to situations in a shy and frightened manner. He was severely depressed. As soon as we returned to the barracks each evening he sat on his bunk and shined his shoes. Within two weeks Horace had worn the bristles off the shoe brush but continued brushing with the flat wooden part. He seldom responded to conversation. Instead he often looked up with glassy, unfocused eyes and stared through you as if you weren't there. When he did speak it was in a shy, muted monotone voice, like a hurt child. That's what he seemed to be, a hurt child.

Then there was Dickie Murtz, the son of a druggist from my home town. He graduated from high school the same year I did and managed to get deferred for the next five years thorough his fathers' political connections. His family had money and political influence. Dickie was a weasel and a habitual whiner. He wept when he was denied a weekend pass to visit his girlfriend. None of us were allowed weekend passes during basic training but Dick knew he was special. He sneaked off base on several weekends to meet with his family who drove down, with his girlfriend, so they could have a tryst. The rest of the troops in our barracks found it disturbing that he got away with it while the rest of us suffered the loneliness of weekends bound to the camp.

Young Billy Barrows had come to us from the Ozarks. He was a light complexioned, rosy cheeked, freckle faced boy who seemed unable to adapt to army life. Billy never showered and had a bad habit of nervously picking his nose and wiping it on his bedding for us to see as we walked by each day. Since he slept in an upper bunk the mess was at eye level to whoever walked past. He was one of the stragglers during any kind of physical activity and had trouble accomplishing combat training tasks. Billy was just a nice, simple backwoods boy who was likeable but annoying. Until he entered military service Billy had had no social interactions with strangers and it showed. The other recruits made fun of him and berated his lack of hygiene. For weeks we all complained to him, to no avail. He responded neither to pleading nor threats. His reaction was always a timid smile and blushing cheeks.

This went on for almost two months. Finally, one day, when his presence was no longer tolerable the guys gave him a GI shower. They forcefully stripped him naked, dragged him to the shower stall and, with stiff bristled GI brushes and hard soap, scrubbed his skin reddish-pink under cold water. He whimpered and cried until it was over, then lay quietly on his bunk mattress, which they had stripped of the filthy sheets and pillowcase.

Billy sulked for days and avoided eye contact with his tormentors. He stopped using his bedding for Kleenex, at least where we could see it, but he still would not shower. Thankfully our basic training stint was almost over and we would have to tolerate him for only a few more days.

10. GRADUATION

At the end of our training program the base sponsored an open visitation day so friends and families could attend our graduation ceremony. Parents and loved ones were welcomed through the gates to spend the day. Picnic tables were set up outdoors. The Companies stood in parade formation while the ceremony took place, proud family members observing. Cadre handed each of us a certificate and a framed photograph of our group, Company 2, smiling, happy, and ready to go home. Afterward we mingled with the visitors.

I excused myself from visiting friends and wandered around saying goodbyes, finding out where some of my buddies were being transferred and introducing myself to their families.

Horace, the shoe brushing recruit, had been given a medical "Section 8" discharge a week earlier. I missed saying goodbye and wishing him well. I felt sorry for him. I imagined he was happy to be back at home.

I avoided Dickie Murtz, the whiner, and his family. I don't know where he went and never saw him again. The last rumor I heard was that his father was pulling some political strings to get the weasel an early discharge.

Billy Barrows, our Ozark boy, sat with his parents and little sister. I walked over and introduced myself. His folks were friendly, warm and loving. Clearly they came from simple means and exuded pure love for their boy. He left for a moment to fetch something from his duffle bag. Since I had deferred induction for five years I was five years older than Billy and many of the other recruits. Perhaps because I appeared older his parents accorded me some sort of senior status. While Billy was gone his mother asked me if Billy had been a good boy and if he had done well. I assured her that she could be proud of him which seemed to please her immensely.

Ralph Madden, the cum laude attorney, was transferring to an Inspector General's office staff in Washington, DC. As we parted he gave me a final kitten imitation and a crooked grin.

Master Sergeant Ciecca, our tough, grizzled old veteran company leader, had mellowed during our last days. I grew to admire and respect him. In recent days he had asked me to help the company clerks with some of their paperwork. I was working in the orderly room early that last morning when he came in. We talked comfortably, no longer master and servant, more like mentor and student.

In a lighthearted, humorous spirit I asked, "Did you know that Ciecca sounds like an Italian word that means "blind," Sergeant?"

"Yeah, I knew that. My folks are from Italy. I've taken a lot of ribbing over my name. Your family's Italian, too, right?"

I said it was. He asked about my plans for the future. I told him I intended to go back home to my engineering job after my two year active duty hitch was up. He smiled and nodded.

"Good. That's good," he said.

I completed my work and rose to leave. He held out his hand and shook mine. "You have a good life. Get married. Have kids. Enjoy life."

This was a warm, almost fatherly side of him I had not glimpsed before today.

"Thanks," I said. Then, on impulse I said, "You're a tough, intimidating guy out there on the training field. I'm glad I got to know you better. You remind me a lot of my own Dad."

He looked at me for a moment, a look of sorrow.

"Funny you should say that," he said. "You remind me of my son."

He ducked his head down. When he looked up at me again his eyes were far away. "He was killed in Korea. He would've been your age now."

Before I could think of what to say he slapped my shoulder, turned his back to me, walked into his office, and closed the door behind him.

Throughout basic training, and again during these last days, most of the college graduates were interviewed by government recruiters who were looking for candidates to become officers, or to join various agencies including the FBI, CIA, Secret Service, Criminal Investigation, et al. Most graduates, like me, steadfastly refused, thinking it was in our best interests to return to civilian life as soon as possible. In retrospect I fear we declined some excellent career opportunities.

Our company received a 30 day furlough. Some drove away by car with their families. Some took the train, departing as they had arrived. Each of us clutched orders telling us where to report for the remainder of our two years of active duty.

Only one of my Fort Dix, Company 2, buddies would show up at my next destination. I would never see or hear from the others again.

RECEPTION STATION
COMPANY 2 26-1 FORT DIX N. J. JANUARY 27 1956

Author, front row, second from right

PART II

Aberdeen Proving Ground

I. The S&P Detachment

Furlough

Our one-month furlough was a chance to go home in uniform and impress our girlfriends, friends and parents, preferably in that order. Despite the frigid March weather I wore a short, Ike jacket, made popular by General Eisenhower during World War II. I could have worn my dress shoes but chose, instead, to wear polished combat boots. With trousers tucked into boots and bloused around the top of the boot—a practice borrowed from airborne paratroopers—my sharpshooter and good conduct medals pinned on the jacket, shiny brass US medallions on collar tips and a garrison cap perched jauntily on a head of bristling short hair I was sure I cut a dashing figure. I selected the garrison cap because it was less formal than the dress cap. It gave the feeling that I was at once a dashing warrior yet the charming boy next door. It could be worn jauntily at what seemed to be the most flattering angle for your hair style. The troops liked this cap and referred to it affectionately as a flight cap, piss-cutter, fore-and-aft cap, envelope cap and a few other unmentionable names due to its resemblance to a part of the female anatomy. I was ready to rumble.

I made the rounds and even managed to visit an old girlfriend I had been interested in during my high school days. She had another boyfriend now but it didn't matter. I knew I made a rakish impression and imagined that she was filled with regret that she had let me get away.

Most of the time was spent with my girlfriend and many of my former coworkers in Syracuse. It was a grand time and the month passed too quickly.

I was soon boarding another train heading south. Unfolding my heavily creased orders I again read my destination: United States Army Ordinance, Ballistics Research Laboratories, Scientific and Professional Detachment, Aberdeen Proving Grounds, Maryland.

The Troops

The Scientific and Professional (S&P) Detachment was comprised of college graduates whose critical skills deferments had expired upon graduation. They were assigned to this unusual group in order to put to good use their educations. They would work on the research and development projects of the Ballistic Research and Nuclear Physics Laboratories (BRL & NPL).

Almost all of the 130 some odd troops in the S&P Detachment at that time had at least a bachelors' degree in one of the sciences. Most had a Masters Degree and some boasted one or more Doctorates in Chemistry, Electronics, Mathematics or Nuclear Physics. A few walked around reading text books full of long numbers and mysterious symbols. Even at the bus stop, in the morning, they stood reading, climbing aboard without looking up from the page. These young men were gifted. With a mere Bachelor of Mechanical Engineering Degree I felt, by comparison, like the village idiot.

Assigning these men to the research laboratories made a lot of sense. It was a good fit. There was, however, one little wrinkle. They were often taken away from their assignments to perform mundane tasks. Although ostensibly assigned full time to various laboratory departments to perform scientific research and development much of their time was spent washing dishes, mopping floors, walking guard posts all night, standing over stockade prisoners with a shotgun and marching in parades. They were taken away from the labs for routine barrack inspections and weekly calisthenics. They pulled KP (Kitchen Police), Guard Duty, Parade Detail and other Battalion tasks for the base.

These frequent interruptions decimated their ability to conduct and complete research and development projects in reasonable time frames. The resulting inefficiencies were demoralizing to these conscientious professionals. Experiments were delayed. Project schedules were impacted. Important test results and reports were postponed.

Thousands of other troops on base were spared from these mundane tasks. For example, there were 16 companies, approximately 4,400 more troops, in the so-called School Troops organization alone. These were exempted from extra duties.

The reason for this apparent misuse of resources was based strictly on the predilection of the Army career officers who controlled the destinies of the S&P detachment. Their extensive military experience gave them a fixed conception of what constituted a good soldier. It precluded objective judgment of the soldier as a scientist and was evidenced by an unfair prejudice against them.

Battalion commander, Major Strange, was a dedicated soldier who declared his distaste for the Scientific and Professional Detachment troops. "I hate S&Ps," he often said publicly. "Damn Joe Colleges!"

His boss, Commanding General Holyfield, was a field promoted product of World War II and the Korean War. This blood and guts commander believed that the S&Ps were unfit for what he called soldiering. He often declared, in parade ground speeches, "These troops WILL soldier, S&P or not!"

While the S&Ps became disheartened they nevertheless did their best to perform well in the laboratories, on KP, Guard Duty, parade activities and Army sports competitions. They participated on post-wide athletic teams and many company level intramural sports teams and won the Post Commander's Sports Trophy two years in a row. They supported all post activities and remained ready to assume assigned duties. There was never a refusal or serious dereliction of duty. These men were not misfits. They were overqualified for garbage detail and underutilized in the laboratories.

To relieve the situation they often relied on a deep and creative sense of humor that showed itself in many ways which included occasional pranks and peccadilloes.

First Platoon barracks, S&P Detachment.

The S&P detachment was housed in several two-story barracks which faced a large, rectangular marching field referred to as the quadrangle. Off to one side of the quadrangle sat Company headquarters. This building had two large rooms, each with a set of stairs leading to its own small porch and entry door. On the left was a recreation room. It held a pool table, ping-pong table, television set and a small mail room for troop use. On the right was the Orderly Room where the Executive Officer (EO), who held the rank of Lieutenant, had his private office. Outside his office sat desks for the First Sergeant, the Duty Sergeant and the Company Clerk.

The quadrangle was where the detachment "fell out" every morning for Reveille, all 130 of them, lining up, shoulder to shoulder, one arms length apart, while the First Sergeant took roll call. Afterward they walked to the mess hall for breakfast, then returned to the barracks to await the bus that would transport them to the laboratories for the work day. The bus returned at noon for lunch and again in the late afternoon when the work day ended. Soldiers who had their own cars were permitted to drive themselves to the lab, though most took the bus to save on fuel costs.

The laboratory work day ended at the same time for troops and civilian government employees alike, around 5 PM.

Soldiers who were assigned to Kitchen Police arose at 3 AM and waited in line at the rear door of the mess hall for the cook to arrive. They worked until well after the last meal was served in the evening.

Those scheduled for Guard Duty reported for inspection in the afternoon, all spiffy and shiny, after which they were given guard post assignments. These lasted, in alternating 4 hour shifts, throughout the night. In the morning they were driven to the post stockade to perform prisoner guard duty all day as well. Guard duty killed two days and one night. It was the most time consuming extra duty on base.

Parade duty involved preparation time, a truck or bus ride to and from wherever the event was to take place, and the parade itself. When held in Baltimore or Washington it killed a full day and night.

Those fortunate enough to be working a normal day at the labs knew that the end of the standard duty day was signaled at 5 PM. That's when the post flag was lowered to the sound of a recorded trumpet playing Retreat, the blast of a cannon, then The National Anthem. It was mandatory that all soldiers, who were outdoors, should stand at attention, face in the direction of the distant flagpole, and hold a salute during the playing of the National Anthem. So, minutes before 5 PM there occurred a scurrying of soldiers for indoor cover of any kind. Inattentive soldiers who had just walked outdoors as the music started wheeled abruptly and darted back indoors.

Corporal Charlie

Corporal Charlie, who liked to be called Chas, lived in the first platoon barrack for a while. He had his own little room, in one corner of the second floor, with a door he could close for privacy. He was not, really, one of the S&Ps. The S&Ps had serial numbers beginning with the letters US signifying that they had been drafted. Some joked that it really stood for Unwilling Servant. Chas' serial number began with RA, which meant Regular Army and indicated he was a volunteer, a career soldier. He was there because he wanted to be. Chas would remain in the army as long as they would have him. He was, by virtue of being a Corporal, higher in rank than many of the S&P newcomers, though he never exerted any real power over them.

Chas served in Korea and bore phosphorous grenade burns on his legs and arms. These refused to heal and were small open sores with white rings around them. He treated these with some kind of ointment but it never seemed to make any difference in their appearance. We liked Chas' from the first morning when he came through, as Reveille played, shouting the now familiar, "Drop your c----s and grab your socks! Get out of those fart sacks! Fall out! Fall out you sorry bastards!" He didn't have to shout out like that but he enjoyed it so much, grinning from ear to ear, that we tolerated it from him.

Chas liked to drink and gamble. On the first Friday after every pay day he would make the rounds of the barrack and ask if we would like to invest in his gambling prowess. He gambled all weekend, slept little, drank heavily and magically appeared on Monday morning for Reveille and roll call. I invested ten dollars once. On Monday he came to me and paid me back my ten plus five dollars as my share of his winnings. That was a fifty percent gain! The next time I loaned him twenty dollars. He lost it all. That put me behind by fifteen dollars. I quit investing then but others continued and claimed they were coming out ahead. Still, over time, only the new arrivals would invest in his gambling skills.

Eventually Chas was transferred to another location and was replaced by a corporal who was more conventional than Charlie.

This one seldom spoke to us, came and went as if he were renting his room from us. We missed Chas.

Now there was no one around who cared enough to wake us, grinning broadly, to the cheerful refrain, "Drop your c----s and grab your socks! Get out of those fart sacks! Fall out! Fall out, you sorry bastards!"

2. The Ballistics Research Laboratories

The Ballistics Research Laboratories (BRL) were made up of a number of individual branches, each pursuing an area of specialization. Each branch was responsible for obtaining and managing project assignments and funding. Progress reports were prepared and reviewed periodically. Many valuable research publications and new or improved weapons systems were forthcoming from this excellent organization. A few anecdotes may serve to give the reader a flavor of life at the research laboratories.

Funding Follies

Once a year each branch submitted a list of possible research projects for consideration by ascending levels of laboratory management and eventually the funding agencies in Washington. There were several unofficial and unspoken axioms at work here that are universal, in one form or another, in every civilian and government organization. It was no different at BRL. There were three cardinal axioms.

Axiom One: *Reviewers always feel obliged to cut or reject something or they won't appear to be doing their jobs.*

So, it makes sense to protect the important projects by offering the reviewers something to cut or reject—a red herring, as it were. This sometimes resulted in very imaginative project ideas deliberately offered as sacrificial lambs for the ever vigilant reviewers.

For example, one proposal stated, correctly, that 80% of the aircraft losses during the Korean War resulted from fuel fires caused by enemy gunfire. The mechanical damage was usually survivable. But it often caused fuel leakage which led to a fuel fire. That is what brought down the aircraft. Therefore, it was proposed, a project should be undertaken to develop a flight maneuver that would take the burning aircraft to a height where there was insufficient oxygen to sustain the fire. The fire would go out. The aircraft would be saved. The program would entail testing jet fuels to establish the altitude at which the burning fuel would extinguish itself. The project was approved by reviewers at each level until someone finally asked, "If you fly high enough to where you don't have enough oxygen to sustain combustion how will the engine stay lit?" That question killed the proposal, as anticipated. The review team had done its job. The important proposals were spared. Everyone was happy.

Axiom Two: *There will always be something you didn't think of—unexpected expenses.*

One way to have extra cash for unexpected expenses is to list the need for new laboratory equipment which you already have from previous programs. You get the money. You don't spend it. But, how will you avoid detection during the annual inspection and inventory visit by the auditors? A double thickness wall with hidden compartments will serve nicely.

Axiom Three: *Any unspent budget will be taken away by the funding agency and will reduce allotments for the next year.*

Got money left over? Buy stuff you may not need now but maybe could use in the future, then store it somewhere. Inside the hollow wall? Or, buy something that one of the other lab departments needs but lacks the money to buy. They will return the favor some day.

Creative budget planning served to adequately fund many highly successful research efforts.

Rockets & Flies

Booster rockets usually use a solid propellant fuel. Most familiar to the public today are the space shuttle launches which include two long, cylindrical solid propellant rockets mounted on either side of the very large liquid fuel main rocket to which the shuttle is directly attached. During launch these two long cylinders ignite along with the main rocket and then separate and fall away in long, smoky arches, part way into the sky.

I was assigned to the Combustion and Incendiary Effects Branch of BRL. Put simply, all projects in this branch were associated with how things burned. My primary project was to optimize the efficiency of solid propellants. This fuel is a dry, highly combustible material that burns in a controlled fashion. The challenge was to find a way to provide a richer oxygen supply to the solid propellant without the use of gases or liquids. One concept was to grind the explosive fuel into a very fine powder, and then to coat each particle with a layer of pure aluminum through a process called vapor deposition. The aluminum coating would oxidize—take on oxygen—when exposed to air, thus coating each particle with an additional source of oxygen. To test the hypothesis we designed a vacuum chamber with small electric heating coils inside. On the coils I placed small pieces of pure aluminum wire. Below the coils sat a small tray holding the white, finely ground explosive powder.

Once everything was prepared inside the vacuum chamber I sealed it and turned on the vacuum pump and waited. It took at least two hours to evacuate the chamber sufficiently. I utilized this time helping with other projects or reading text books related to our work.

After evacuating the vacuum chamber, a small motor was turned on which vibrated the powder tray so the particles would jiggle and rotate and receive an evenly distributed coating of aluminum. The heating coils were then turned on to vaporize the aluminum wire.

When the aluminum had vaporized and deposited itself on the powder the system was shut down, the powder removed and exposed to air. The thin, almost mono-molecular aluminum coating would then oxidize.

The finished powder was compressed into small pellets. These pellets were ignited and the resulting combustion event, if any, was photographed for study with a high speed Schlieren camera.

The Schlieren camera took photos of explosions that took place inside a thick-walled, steel reinforced, concrete bunker. The camera employed a rapidly rotating carousel of mirrors that beamed a series of still images across a covered strip of film. When the carousel was at full speed a button was pushed which simultaneously caused the shutter to open and the explosive to ignite. Thus one could photograph, for example, a stick of exploding dynamite and get a series of still photographs showing the progression of the combustion or flame front along the stick.

The bunker sat against one wall of a large laboratory room. Engineers in this room could safely watch through a heavy, firebrick glass porthole in the wall of the bunker. The small concrete room in which I worked to develop a better solid propellant shared a common wall with the bunker. While I worked on one side of the wall other scientists sometimes conducted explosive tests on the opposite side.

Prior to each test a siren wailed three times as a warning. The mirrored carousel of the Schlieren camera would begin its spin, building up speed until it hit the desired revolutions per second. Moments later the explosion would occur.

I usually left my small test cell when I heard the warning, but if I was in the middle of a critical point in my work I simply covered my ears and waited. The concussion caused a shock wave that whipped my trousers smartly around my legs. My ears rang for a time. Then an all-clear siren sounded.

On occasion, when I ran out of reading material but could not leave the evacuating system unattended, I was forced to patiently stare at the equipment, listen to the vacuum pump and watch the vacuum meter slowly move. Sitting there, unable to leave, with nothing to do for the moment, I became intrigued by the ubiquitous Maryland horse flies. One or two of these big, black, noisy, creatures often zipped about the room, hovered about my head and then landed momentarily on the desk, the vacuum chamber or my arms.

The inquisitive mind of the researcher kicked in. The flies were easy to catch and imprison under an inverted beaker. Using a Q tip or toothpick I placed a drop of one of the many chemicals we kept available, such as acetone or laboratory alcohol, on a piece of paper towel and slid it under the beaker. Thus I collected data on which liquids attracted the flies, which repelled them and how much the flies could tolerate. Alcohol yielded the most intriguing results. A drunken horse fly behaved incredibly similar to an inebriated human; walking unsteadily, staggering and occasionally bumbling into the beaker walls. However, if overdosed, the fly stumbled with increasingly erratic movements then, with resignation, flopped onto its back and expired. At least, I assumed they expired. I threw them outside. Perhaps they slept it off and awoke with a hangover.

Shape Charges & Notebooks

Stan Polaski was a tall, gangly and delightfully unsophisticated soldier with a wife waiting for him back home. With his occasional weekend pass he drove to Pennsylvania to spend a couple days with his family. His fellow researcher and constant companion was Bob Dailey. Both men had been inducted after graduating from the same college.

They were a study in opposites. Stan was inclined to be proper in dress and comportment, a little shy and introverted. Bob was an animated version of the cartoon army character "Sad Sack." Stan was shy and reserved, with a timid smile that emerged when the more extroverted Bob pulled some practical joke on him. Their banter was clever and entertaining to watch. More outgoing and inclined to suffer mishaps, Bob could always be counted on for a laugh. Both held Master's degrees in metallurgy. Both were assigned to Second Platoon, in the S&P Detachment.

Bob complained nightly about Stan's snoring. Awakened suddenly one night by an unusually loud snort from Stan, Bob sat bolt upright, spun to his right to face the noise, lost his balance in the darkness and fell with his right hand plunging into the icky cold water and cigarette stubs in the butt can sitting on the floor between the bunks.

Stan's lab project involved improving the effectiveness of something called a shaped charge. This device contains an explosive charge that is shaped to focus the effect of the explosive's energy. Various types are used to initiate nuclear weapons, penetrate heavy armor and can be used for commercial purposes in the oil and gas industry. A typical, modern, lined shaped charge can penetrate armor steel to a depth of 10 or more times the diameter of the charge's cone. The weapon makes an excellent tank and bunker killer.

Stan had arrived at Aberdeen a year before I did and had been working on the one project all that time. With each trial his results improved. At the conclusion of his two year duty Stan had made impressive improvements in the effectiveness of shaped charges for specific special targets.

One Friday afternoon Stan had almost completed a series of 30 test explosions taking careful data and notations on this final and possibly conclusive series. Bob and I had come to watch as Stan set up what he felt would be his final and triumphant test. All his prior tests suggested that this metallurgical combination would produce a vastly improved result. He would complete the series today and have the weekend to celebrate. With just fifteen minutes left in the day Stan hurried to finish this final data point.

We watched as he quickly mounted the test specimen in the bunker, making rapid notations in his project notebook as he worked. We tried to stay out of his way, getting closer only when Stan asked for help. He checked the camera, making sure the film was properly loaded and ready. He hurried us out of the bunker, closed and locked the heavy door. We stepped back as he turned on the camera. A civilian technician hit the button that sounded the loud warning siren which was broadcast on loudspeakers throughout the lab buildings and outdoor areas. The camera's mirrored carousel began spinning. A meter on the control panel indicated its speed in revolutions per minute. The technician stood at the firing panel, one eye on the camera speed indicator, one hand on the large, red firing button. When the mirror carousel was at speed the technician began a countdown.

"This is it," Stan said, "The last one." He nodded at the technician who depressed the firing button. A powerful, muffled "Boom" sent vibrations and a small shock wave through the room. We waited another few minutes for the mirror carousel to wind down. With just a couple minutes remaining—just long enough to tidy up and walk out to the bus—Stan opened the door and walked briskly in, followed closely by Bob and me. I bumped into Bob's back as he slammed into Stan who had stopped dead in his tracks.

"Aw, nooo!!" Stan wailed.

Bob leaned to his left, I to my right, as we peered around Stan's shoulders to see what had paralyzed him. Tiny bits of paper, like little snowflakes, fluttered slowly through the air, drifting to the floor. Scattered around the shed were pieces of Stan's precious project notebook. In his excitement to complete the test series before the end of the day and the week he had inadvertently left the notebook leaning against the shaped charge. We looked at one another for a quiet moment. Stan began to pick up pieces of the notebook. Small bits, like confetti, still floated about the bunker. Bob and I tried to help but before long we were leaning helplessly against each other, holding tattered notebook remnants, laughing while Stan stared off into space.

Stan doesn't talk much about it. He turns a fiery red when, as we board the bus at the end of each day, someone asks him, "Hey, Stan. Blow up any notebooks today?"

Spesutie Island

Aberdeen Proving Grounds is located on the shores of Chesapeake Bay. It is a large, natural meadowland which is home to much wildlife including an abundance of deer. At the farthest border with the water is Spesutie Road. It crosses a narrow wooden bridge leading to Spesutie Island. The bridge is guarded by a Military Police post because the island holds additional, research facilities. On this island were several trailers equipped with electronics and test facilities for highly classified work.

Specialist Third Class Dennis Shorefield held an advance degree in Nuclear Physics and was assigned to the Nuclear Physics Laboratories. On occasion he conducted tests in one of the trailers on Spesutie Island. A short, chubby guy with a perpetual frown of concentration, Denny loved his work. He was often one of the last to leave when they closed the trailers each day. He soon tired of being rushed to leave with the others on the bus and one day decided to drive his own car. Parking his car outside the trailer he kept working after all the others had left for the night. He told us he would be back before the mess hall closed. By 8:30 his buddies became concerned and contacted the Military Police. The MPs said they would send a car in to look for him.

Dennis had finished his last set of data points and closed down his test equipment for the night. He put on his jacket and fatigue cap, picked up his books, turned out the lights and walked out the door, turning back to lock it. That's when he heard the heavy breathing.

He turned to look into the darkness and saw several sets of eyes glowing in the deep shadows around his car. He froze. The eyes moved and multiplied, staring at him, and then approached the small porch on which he still stood, paralyzed. As they closed on him he finally reacted, spinning back to the door, jamming the key into the lock, twisting it open. He heard claws clattering up the short steps.

Four MPs arrived later in two cars and saw the darkened trailer in their headlights as they turned into the gravel driveway. Dennis' car was nearby. They turned on a spot-light, shined it on and around Dennis' car but saw nothing. As the lights panned to the trailer there was a flurry of furtive movement. On the steps and porch of the trailer milled a pack of wild dogs. The MPs blew the car horns, shouted and played the spotlights on the pack. The dogs, moving to escape from the glare, trotted down the steps and reluctantly circled behind Dennis' car. Leaving the motors running and the lights on the MPs got out of their cars carrying night sticks and flashlights, shouting and waving arms as they approached the pack which turned and disappeared into the blackness of the night. They searched around the car and checked inside it. They found nothing. They headed back to the trailer.

The trailer door cracked open and a cautious Dennis stepped out. He had been watching through the window. He thanked his rescuers for their help, locked the door behind him and ducked into his own car. The vehicles drove in a caravan back to the bridge, past the guard shed, through the gate and off Spesutie Island.

We had been warned not to linger on Spesutie Island after dark. Now we found out why. During World War II this island served as an embarkation point for soldiers leaving Aberdeen for war in the European theatre. American troops, like many others, had acquired pets, usually dogs. They were not allowed to take them on the ships and were forced to abandon them on the island. These former pets had grown into a formidable wild pack that successfully hunted small game and the occasional deer. They roamed the island after dark.

They had grown aggressive and, it appeared, would not hesitate to hunt a lone human being. Poor, corpulent Dennis, who may have looked like Thanksgiving Dinner to the pack, always left the island on the bus, with the other troops, from that day forward.

3. THE TRAINED KILLER

The summer weather in Maryland, at least in this part of Maryland, is conducive to all manner of insects and bugs—June bugs in particular. When June days are hot and muggy they swarm, flying and crawling around during the day, assailing windows and porch lights by the thousands at night. When the occasional one slipped inside the barrack past the screen door it would buzz noisily and ricochet around until someone got up from their bunk, captured it and threw it out the door.

One night, just after lights out, as we lay in our bunks, I heard the loud buzz of a June bug whirring near me. I swung my arm blindly in the half light coming in the window from the porch fire light and luckily knocked it to the floor next to me where it lay, stunned, on its back.

Jim, whose bunk was clear across the barrack from mine, called out, "Guess you're gonna have to throw it out."

I leaned over the edge and saw it lying there on its back, long black plastic looking legs waving helplessly. With the back of my hand I gave it a sharp hockey slap shot, sending it sliding, like a hockey puck, across the linoleum floor. It stopped directly under Jim's cot. He promptly slapped it back to me. We were both too lazy to get up and toss it out so the game continued for a while. The sound of its hard shell skidding back and forth on the linoleum finally stopped when my bad shot sent the stunned bug sailing under one of the other bunks with a soundly sleeping occupant. It remained there, unconscious or playing "possum" to arise later and torment the boys nearby with its noisy, buzzing wings.

On pleasant summer days we often ate lunch at the picnic tables outside the labs. One day, Bob, Stan, Robert P., Gerry M. and I sat eating lunch amidst the June bugs. They filled the air around us, several crawling on the table. We casually brushed them off if they got too close to our food, or plinked them across the table and off the edge.

"God, I hate these bugs," said Stan. "Ya wonder why God made them."

"What good are they?" asked Bob.

"Maybe birds eat them," speculated Robert P.

"I haven't seen any birds eating them," I offered.

"They are edible, y'know," Gerry M. said. "The larvae and the adults have lots of protein."

Gerry, who had a degree in Chemical Engineering, had taken advanced survival training at a camp in Georgia before coming to Aberdeen. He was showing off.

"How do you know?" asked Robert P.

"Cause I've eaten them during survival training."

"Yeah, right," I said.

"I did! It's called the Green Beetle, or genus Cotinis, species C.nitida!"

Man, I hated it when Gerry flaunted his knowledge.

"Eat one now!"

"Make it worth my while," he answered.

"Whattaya mean?" asked Stan.

"I'll eat one for five bucks."

We looked at each other. Gerry M. had a habit of exaggerating his exploits. We had good reason to suspect that he wouldn't eat one, probably never had. I pulled out a buck and a quarter, followed by the others. We slapped our money on the table.

"There you go," I taunted. "Down the hatch!"

We waited as Gerry picked up the $5.00 and stuffed it into his pocket. He put the last bite of his sandwich into his mouth, chewing slowly. Then, as we watched, Gerry caught a good sized June bug. He held it in his closed fist for a while, swallowing the last bite of his sandwich. He took a drink of his soda. I thought he was stalling and would back down. He opened his hand, palm up.

We stared at the huge beetle with its greenish brown shell, small bulbous head, and long black legs that crawled slowly across his palm. He continued to hold it just long enough to build up our suspense, then popped it into his mouth. I heard the crunch and pop as he bit down, then watched in amazement as he slowly chewed and swallowed it. He picked up his can of soda and took a long swig.

Robert P. made a sour face and asked, "What does it taste like?"

"Oranges," Gerry replied. "Not bad; a little sweet with a touch of citric."

"Man," Bob said, "I didn't think you'd do it. I'm impressed."

Gerry grinned, "Hell, man, I'm not just a pretty face! I'm a trained killer!"

We all laughed. During basic training we were often reminded of this.

In the immortal words of one of our tough basic training drill Sergeants, "You gonna cost the gummint twenny thowsen dollahs ta become trained killahs! We gonna teach you a lotta ways ta kill da enemy befo' he kills you! You gonna leave here a warriah, a trained killah! Gonna come a time when you life gonna depend on it, so pay attenshun!"

We learned at Aberdeen Proving Ground that all recruits from every basic training camp had received the same admonition in much the same wording. So, it was not uncommon for the GIs to joke about being trained killers.

"Yep, guess you really are," we chimed in agreement.

It was only a few months later, in early Fall, that Gerry M. took a cab into Aberdeen to see a movie. It was dark when he came out. He walked to the local diner for a hamburger, fries and coffee, then took a cab back to the base. Taxis with special permits were allowed to drive in and out of the base. This one was driven by a woman cabby. As they approached the Military Police guard shack she slowed under the lights and waved at the MP who glanced at her window sticker and waved her on through. Without stopping she accelerated into the dark, unlit roadway when something large loomed out of the darkness just feet in front of her headlights. A loud thump was followed by breaking glass and the screech of tires as she slammed on the brakes.

"Holy geez, what was that?" she asked.

"I think it was a deer," Gerry answered. "Here comes the MP."

The MP ran up and motioned for the cabby to lower her window. "You hit a deer. Please step out of the car and give me a hand."

They got out and stood staring at the badly injured doe. She was bleating pitifully in obvious pain.

"We got to get her out of the road so other cars can pass. Give me a hand here."

They grabbed legs and ears and pulled the suffering beast to one side of the road.

"What do we do now?" she asked.

"I've got to call it in and report it." He took the driver's information including her base pass. "Wait here."

He walked back to the shack and used the phone, then returned.

"OK. Someone will come in the morning to get the carcass. Guess you can leave now." He handed her paperwork back to her and turned to leave.

"Wait a minute!" she called out to him. "We can't let her lay here all night suffering like this!"

"Yeah," agreed Gerry, "Someone ought to put her out of her misery."

The creature was bleating even more now in agony and terror, her legs thrashing in a futile attempt to rise. "What do you want me to do?" the MP asked. "I'm not going to use my weapon to kill it. I'd get in trouble."

"Wait," she said, turning to her cab and opening the door. From beneath the driver's seat she pulled out a leather handled knife with a 12 inch, double edged blade that glinted in the headlights of the cab.

"Use this and cut its throat."

The MP stepped back from it as if it were a poisonous snake.

"Not me." He turned to Gerry. "This is your cab ride, soldier. Guess you get to do it."

The cabby handed the knife to Gerry. "Here you go, big boy. Just pull its head back and give it a quick slice, hard and deep. She'll bleed out in a minute and it'll be over."

Gerry held the knife in his hands, staring at it. He tried to remember what we had been taught. Come up from behind, reach over the top of the enemy's head, grab the front edge of the helmet, pull it up hard to raise the chin, slash with the right hand across the throat. But, the helmet might not be strapped. You could be left with a handful of helmet. It's much safer to grab the enemies chin, lift and slash. Better yet, insert the blade into the spine in the nape of the neck or near the tailbone, then twist the blade upward. That would kill instantly. No screaming that way. He wondered if he could stick the blade into the spine near the back of the head. He didn't know if it worked the same on deer. He decided to slit the deer's throat. Cut the carotid artery.

He stepped off the road and around the poor creature. He stood behind the head and reached down with his left hand and grabbed the muzzle. It flinched and cried out in fear. He gripped the knife handle, then shifted it and held it, poised, his arm outstretched. He hesitated again, then, he saw her eyes, filled with fear. She looked back up at him.

Without looking up he let go of her muzzle. Her head dropped to the ground.

"Oh for Christ sake! Gimme that!" the lady cabby said, snatching the knife from his hand.

She took a large step over the deer's body, hooked the chin upward with her left hand and expertly pulled the blade across the throat all in one swift motion. Blood spurted a yard out and pulsed rapidly. The doe made horrible gurgling sounds and thrashed her legs furiously for a minute or two, then lay still. The blood flow slowed to a drizzle.

Gerry was shaken. The MP looked at her admiringly. "Where did you learn how to do that?"

"Hell!" she said. "I been hunting deer since I was a kid. Dad and I use to dress 'em out in the field. Piece o' cake."

"Get in the cab soldier," she said, wiping the blade and her hands on an oily rag she took from the trunk. "I'll take you the rest of the way in."

A few minutes later Gerry walked, zombie like, into the barracks.

"How was the movie?" I asked.

He told me about the doe.

"It was awful to watch. But you know the worst part? I'm a warrior. I've had Twenty Thousand Dollars worth of training. I'm a trained killer! But I couldn't do it. I had to have a woman do it for me."

The next day, at lunch it was all we talked about. Gerry smiled, leaned back, hands clasped behind his head and said, philosophically, "Well, one thing I've learned. It's a lot easier to eat a June bug than to kill a living creature with big brown eyes."

And we all agreed, again.

4. Radar Signals & Butt Cans

The barracks were cookie cutter identical. Indoors each wall was lined with wall lockers, one on each side of each window. Beneath each window a simple table hung from the wall at window sill level. In front of each wall locker was an army bunk. A heavy bar spanned the space between wall lockers. Long, zippered clothing bags were hung from these bars. In front of each bunk sat a foot locker. Sitting on the floor of the aisle, about every second bunk, was a red butt can. These were used coffee cans, painted red, with an inch of water in them. They were used for the disposal of cigarette butts. The layout arrangement allowed each soldier to have his own bunk, foot locker, clothing bags, wall locker, window and writing table.

Army Regulations designate exactly how every square inch of flat space was to be used. Every soldier's foot locker kept socks in exactly the same place as every other soldier's foot locker. Every wall locker held exactly the same things in the same spots.

There was one space in each wall locker and each foot locker that was designated as "personal," which meant the soldier could put something of a personal nature in that spot. This could be a photo or souvenir rock, for example.

Many of us had a small lamp and radio on the writing table. On evenings and weekends one or more radios were turned on softly playing music while soldiers relaxed or wrote letters.

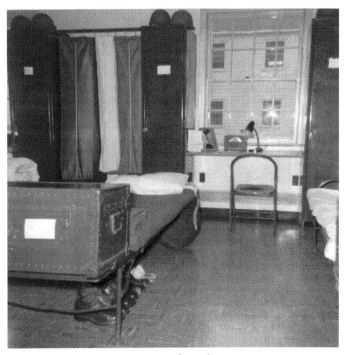

Home away from home.

Our barrack was one of a dozen located around a quadrangle-shaped field. Behind the first platoon barrack was a radar station with a large, rotating dish that, when operating, emitted a continuous, repetitive radar signal. During those times it was impossible to listen to a radio because the radar signal could be heard, over the radio, as a piercing "chirp-chirp—chirrrrrp......chirp-chirp—chirrrrrp." It was maddening.

The men soon discovered that a metal object, such as our cigarette butt cans, placed in just the right spot between the radio and the radar station, would reflect the radar away and the nerve jangling sound would stop..........unless I was lying on my bunk with nothing to do.

Through practice I had learned how to produce an exact duplicate of the radar signal by whistling through a small gap in my two front teeth with little movement of the lips.

One slow Sunday afternoon Vincent Pisante turned on his radio to soft background music while he sat at his table composing a letter to his girlfriend in California. Vinny was a short, rather good looking, always neatly dressed kid from Los Angeles. He liked to write with his radio playing classical music. His bunk and table were across the aisle from me. I could watch him as I lay back on my bunk. Pavarotti was singing the exquisitely beautiful aria, Nessun Dorma, from Pucini's opera, Turnadot.

The radar station suddenly activated interrupting Pavarotti with its "chirp-chirp—chirrrrrrp.......chirp-chirp—chirrrrrrp." I lay still, watching from the corner of my eye as Vinny got up, walked to the main aisle, picked up a butt can, placed it on his writing table and shifted it around until the signal stopped. Pavarotti continued. Vinny picked up his pen and began writing again, the music gently filling the air.

I waited until he was engrossed mid-sentence in his writing, then began my perfect imitation, "chirp-chirp—chirrrrrp...... chirp-chirp—chirrrrrp."

He lay down his pen and moved the can slightly. I stopped whistling. Again Vinny picked up his pen, sighed deeply, hunched over the desk and began writing. A moment later I started; "chirp-chirp—chirrrrrp......chirp-chirp—chirrrrrp."

Vinny put down his pen and taking the butt can in both hands began shifting it around. I stopped but now the can was out of the line of fire from the radar station and his radio began to pick up the real signal from the radar, "chirp-chirp—chirrrrrp......chirp-chirp—chirrrrrp."

This went on for some time. Each time he got the can in the right location and the radar signal was interrupted I waited until he had resumed writing. Then when he seemed engrossed enough I began my imitation. Finally, trembling with rage, Vinny slammed down his pen, turned off the radio and stormed out of the barracks leaving a trail of foul language. I spent many a pleasant weekend afternoon tormenting one or another of my barrack-mates thusly.

Until one day when Jim Gateway walked into the barracks while I was seriously messing with another guys head, alternating my whistles with the radar station signal.

Jim was a tall, slightly pudgy, Negro gentleman from North Carolina who held a PhD in Mathematics, had a very sensitive nature and was easy to like. He spent a lot of his spare time reading and sleeping. Now, he stood in the center aisle between bunks, watched and listened to the strange behavior of the radar signal and the frustrated victim's attempt to block it with a butt can. This had happened to Jim in the past and remained an unsolved mystery. With his sharp mental acuity, Jim reasoned it out. I was the only other person in the room. The radar could be seen out the nearby window. The behavior of the signal was irrational. After a while Jim came to me. He sat on the edge of the bunk next to where I was innocently reclining.

Smiling, he leaned forward and whispered, "You stop messin' with me when I want to hear my radio and we can keep this between us."

"Done," I said.

And so, for many months, on weekend afternoons, Jim Gateway's radio was the only one that did not experience the strange radar signal that mysteriously penetrated the protection of the butt can.

5. GOING TO THE MOVIES

With the occasional weekend pass I was able to visit family and friends up in upstate New York. One weekend I returned with my own car, driving madly all Sunday night to return arriving half an hour before Reveille on Monday morning. This was my first car and she occupied a special place in my heart. I did much of my own maintenance on it in the next months and affectionately referred to her as Hunk O' Junk or 'HOJ'.

I sometimes used my permanent day pass and HOJ to visit the town of Aberdeen or nearby Havre de Grace, evenings and weekends, for a movie or to get civilian food.

My first visit to the only drive-in theatre in Aberdeen was memorable. Stan, Bob and I went to see Moby Dick with Gregory Peck as Captain Ahab. We crowded into the front seat of HOJ as the film started. Settling in with our drinks and food we kicked back.

I noticed movement out of the corner of my eye and glanced into the car to my left. A couple was necking heavily. This was not an uncommon activity at drive-in movies so I turned my attention back to the screen for a few minutes. Then I looked to my left again. There was a lot of movement, shifting positions, steamy windows. I tried to keep up with the story on the big screen in front of me but finally gave up when the couple disappeared from view and there was only the periodic appearance of a bare rump popping into view.

When our neighbors were sitting upright again I turned to Stan and asked, "What did I miss?"

"What do you mean?" he asked back.

"I wasn't looking. What did I miss?" I repeated.

"Did you fall asleep?" Bob queried.

"No, I was the watching a couple having sex in the next car."

Now both of them looked away from the screen and became agitated.

"Why didn't you tell us? What happened? What did you see?"

"I didn't want to interrupt your movie. So, tell me, what did I miss?"

"No," they insisted, "You tell us what we missed!"

So that was how we spent the next half hour. I had to repeat, in detail, what I had seen. As their astonishment grew I felt inexplicably compelled to fabricate what I had seen. With each expression of awe and teenage breathlessness I got from them the fabrication grew. It became more torrid with each answered question. By the time I was done with my creation Stan and Bob could hardly contain their excitement and envy. The movie was forgotten.

We left the drive-in, stopped at the local diner for a cup of coffee, and drove back to the barracks. This adventure was retold by them, growing like a living thing. It became a legend among the barracks which, I am sure, sold a lot of drive-in tickets the following weekends.

Me and HOJ

My first visit to the walk-in movie theatre in Aberdeen was also memorable but for a totally different reason. I went with another buddy, Anthony, who came from a farm in Alabama. Anthony was not a member of the S&P detachment. He was a Military Policeman I had befriended at a local bar in nearby Havre de Grace. He had already put in three years at APG and would soon have to decide whether to re-enlist or go home to the family business.

Anthony had a deep southern drawl that was replete with local idioms. As we drove off the base he looked up at the sky which was covered with dark, billowing, angry looking clouds. He gave his head a slow shake and said, "Mmmm, mmmm! It's gonna rain like a cow pissin' on a flat rock!" And, you know, I could envision that and knew exactly how hard a rainfall that was going to be.

On this Friday night we had found ourselves with no plans for the weekend and no assigned duties, so we impulsively drove into town. He spotted the theatre marquee and suggested we take in a movie. We got tickets and as we walked in I noticed a small stairway going upstairs. A red velvet rope was clipped across the bottom step.

"Where do you suppose that goes?" I asked.

"To the balcony," he whispered.

I noticed that the theatre was small and thought it might be neat to see the screen from up there so I started toward the stairs. He grabbed my arm.

"No," he hissed, "You can't go up there."

He moved me down the aisle. I knew Anthony had been to this theatre many times before so I surmised the balcony was closed for a good reason. But, from time to time I thought I heard noises from the balcony. For a while I dismissed the noises as my imagination or, perhaps, tricks of the particular acoustics of this theatre. Finally, I was sure I was hearing sounds of voices and movement.

I leaned over and whispered, "Somebody is upstairs. I can hear them. How come they can go up there and we can't?" I asked.

"Them are negrahs," he replied, "They can't sit down here with the whites. They have to sit up there."

I was dumbstruck. I was from upstate New York. We didn't have many black people in my home town but the few we had were free to do anything the whites did. One of my childhood friends was a tall black boy who used to come to my house early in the morning and walk with me to school. We were friends for years. I was speechless by what Anthony had just said and could only think the equivalent of "Wow!"

Later on, as I lived among the people in that area and came to know them better I became aware of a much stronger segregation sentiment, not just on the part of the whites, but on the part of the blacks as well. Old battle lines still existed from years gone by.

Perhaps it was a defense mechanism on both sides, but it was undeniable. Inevitably I came to accept it as the norm. It was the local culture.

In the Spring of 1957 I took a leave and drove HOJ to Florida for a week. On the way south I passed through a small town in the Carolinas. The road made a sharp 90 degree left turn at the leading edge of the town. There, directly in front of me, was a huge billboard, three feet tall, ten feet wide. Big black letters on a white background said, "Keep Moving Nigger!"

A strange sense of uneasiness crept over me and though the sign was not directed toward me I was compelled to keep moving until that town was far behind me.

6. THE HAPPY CLAM

After the movie Anthony took me to a bar called The Happy Clam a few miles south of Aberdeen. It sat on a spit of land off Route 40 that stuck out into the Bush River which curved around the southern border of Aberdeen Proving Grounds and emptied into Chesapeake Bay. The bar was a small, one room shack-like structure that sat on the edge of a marshy beach. Inside were half a dozen small tables with chairs and sawdust on the worn wooden floor.

Tommy and Pearl, a young, married couple, owned the place. Tommy was an ex sailor with tattooed arms and a barrel chest. Pearl was a very pretty brunette with long hair, dark eyes, an attractive figure and deep dimples. She had a small anchor tattoo on one arm, just below her left shoulder. They looked like a couple that would own a small beer bar on the beach. Anthony had known them for all of his three years at Aberdeen. He thought of them as long time friends.

A juke box rested in one corner. On the counter was a large jar of pickled eggs and another with huge dill pickles. Each jar bore a hand printed sign that advertised "$1.00 each." A pair of tongs sat on a chipped plate that sat between the jars.

Anthony introduced me to Tommy and Pearl and said "Ya gotta try those pickled eggs. Pearl makes 'em herself." I bought one and it was good with a cold mug of draft beer.

Just before closing Tommy invited us to their house to play cards and visit. It was a summer cottage, just a short walk across the sand, with a screened in porch that faced the water. Pearl, Anthony and I went on ahead while Tommy stayed behind to close up the bar. Pearl broke out a six pack of beer and a deck of playing cards. We sat at the kitchen table and she dealt.

"So, Anthony, tell us about that USO dancer you met last month. How's that goin'?" Pearl asked.

"Oh, yeah," he replied. "Her name's Carol!"

Once he started talking about her he became animated with excitement. He had really fallen for her in a big way. They danced well together, had a lot of the same interests and she really cared about him. They had already talked about maybe getting married. He could re-enlist, maybe get a promotion to Sergeant and they would live near the base in a small apartment.

Eventually Tommy showed up and we spent most of the night playing cards, drinking Tommy's beer and just having a great time. By early dawn Tommy had crashed, Anthony was glassy eyed and Pearl and I were the only ones still talking clearly but a lot slower.

After that weekend a ritual developed. Anthony and I went to the Clam after dinner every Friday evening and stayed until closing, then walked over to Tommy and Pearl's house, played cards, drank beer and listened to Anthony describe his growing love affair with Carol.

Pearl warned him that some of the local gals were pretty desperate to escape from the small town and were looking hard to find someone to take them away from this army base environment. But Anthony was sure she was different. He proudly showed us her picture. She was a pretty blue-eyed blonde whose smile showed dazzling white teeth and deep dimples. Anthony had purchased an engagement ring and planned to take his annual furlough soon. He would propose next week. She would go home with him to meet his family. He decided he would not re-enlist in the army. He'd help his Dad run the family farm. The farm was a big supplier for one of the major producers of meat and pork products. Anthony was one happy guy.

Then he disappeared.

I didn't see Anthony all week on base. He wasn't in his barracks when I drove over on the next Friday night. I went to The Happy Clam. Tommy and Pearl had not heard from him. We visited, went to the house, played cards, drank beer and speculated on Anthony's whereabouts. Our guess was that Anthony had proposed, Carol had accepted and they had gone to Alabama to meet his family.

The next Friday night I again went to the Happy Clam, sat on a stool at the bar, ordered a draft beer and one pickled egg from Tommy and was happy as a clam myself until Pearl came over and sat next to me.

"I have a friend who works the Aberdeen USO," she said. "She knows Carol and she met Anthony a couple times."

I waited for her to continue.

"Anthony proposed to Carol last week and gave her the ring. She was pretty excited about it. He told Carol about the farm, told her that after they were married they would move to the farm, with his folks, and help them run the place. He said they would inherit the whole shebang when his Dad retired, which wouldn't be long now 'cause his Dad was ready to chuck it in as soon as Anthony could take it on. Then he showed her pictures of the place. He was so proud of the spread – acres of pig pens and feed troughs. Well, Carol gave him back the ring and told him she wasn't gonna be a pig farmer's wife. He begged her but she said she'd live as the wife of a measly army Sergeant but sure as hell not on a pig farm. She gave him back the ring and got up and left. I guess he was pretty broken up. They haven't seen Anthony at the USO since."

I, too, never saw Anthony again. He did take that furlough but decided not to re-enlist. He went home to the Alabama pig farm and never came back. Every time I see big, black, ominous rain clouds I think of Anthony and cows and flat rocks.

Strangely enough I saw a movie, some years later, about a young Officer candidate who proposed to a local young lady and was rejected, like Anthony, when she learned her beau was leaving the military and returning to run his father's farm. In the movie the young man committed suicide.

Anthony just went home.

7. First Christmas

It was late December, 1956. My first Christmas at Aberdeen was a day away and a lot of the troops had taken furlough time. Three-day passes were issued to many others. In another couple days the base would empty out with the population reduced to those who had duty assignments or those who, for reasons of their own, chose not to leave. The labs were about to close down for the holidays.

That morning Ed Paisly, our branch chief, told us we could take the afternoon off and start the Holiday weekend early. Just before lunch Tom Metzger, our senior civilian, called me on the phone extension out in my little vacuum chamber work cell.

"Time to quit for the day," he said. "Come on in, if you can stay for a little while."

I had driven my car to work that day, so I didn't have to hurry to catch a ride. Also, I had Guard Duty during that coming weekend and wasn't going anywhere for the holiday.

As I walked in I saw the four civilian employees of our department, Tom, Josh, Art, and Ony sitting around the conference table.

"Got time for a Christmas toddy?" Tom asked.

"Sure," I answered, "What do we have?"

Tom lifted a bottle of pure laboratory grade ethanol—200 proof stuff.

"Here are some quarters," he said turning to me with outstretched hand. "Go down the hall and buy three bottles of Coke from the machine."

When I got back I saw five clean, empty, graduated beakers sitting in front of Tom. He filled each half way with Ethanol and topped each off with an equal amount of cold Coca Cola. We each took one and raised them in salutation. We were holding, in our hands, a lethal sized 100 proof cocktail.

"Merry Christmas gents!" Tom declared.

We clinked beakers as we repeated, in unison, "Merry Christmas!!"

It was the smoothest drink I ever tasted. Like liquid gold it slipped over the tongue and soon produced a warm, mellow happiness. We sipped and talked and laughed. With much back slapping and wishes for the New Year we locked up and left for our individual abodes. I felt fine, clear headed, happy but not the least bit intoxicated. The drive back to the barracks was uneventful. Few cars remained on base so the streets were empty. I parked in the lot behind my barrack. As I walked into the rear door I saw Bernie Hoefner about to go out the front door.

Looking back over his shoulder he shouted, "Hey, you better hurry. The last mail call is early today. They're closing down for the holiday weekend."

I scurried after him and walked across the quadrangle to our company headquarters building, which housed the Orderly Room and, next door, the Recreation Room. Tucked in one corner of the Recreation Room was a small cubicle with a barred window. This was the mail room. A line had formed from the window back around the pool table, the ping-pong table and out the door. As each soldier got to the window he spoke his last name to the clerk. The clerk turned back, scanned the alphabetized pigeon holes, sorted through and turned back with mail or a quick, "Nothing today."

It took me a long time to work my way up to the window. As the guy in front of me took his mail and stepped to one side I placed my hands on the window sill and said my name. The clerk turned to the pigeon holes to look for my mail.

I was still smiling and feeling just fine when, without warning, my legs disappeared. Well, not really, but they simply collapsed. I was on both knees, arms raised above my head, fingertips clutching the window sill. The clerk turned back to the window, his hand outstretched with my mail. He saw no one standing there. I was out of his line of sight. Then he noticed my fingers still clinging to the window sill. He swung the bars open and leaned out to look down. I stared upward at his puzzled face.

He grinned and asked, "What are ya' doin' down there?"

All I could do, with a little help from the guy behind me, was to pull myself back to my feet and say, "Damned if I know!"

That was my first encounter with the effects of pure laboratory grade ethanol mixed 50/50 with Coca Cola.

It was also my last.

8. HAVRE DE GRACE

One summer Saturday Stan, Bob and I drove the 4.8 miles north of Aberdeen to the small town of Havre de Grace. It sits snugly at the mouth of the Susquehanna River where it empties into Chesapeake Bay. Started by John Smith in 1608 Havre de Grace almost became the capital of our nation. It lost to Washington, DC by one vote. With one more vote it could have become an overgrown, crowded, poverty stricken, crime infested, tourist crawling megalopolis inhabited by questionable politicians and their cronies. Instead, by one lucky vote it remained a quaint little town with a police force of about three cops, a theatre, some small stores, one grade school, one high school and a large park that slopes gently down from the street to the waters' edge.

In the park we found a statue of a gentleman named John O'Neil. He was a member of the local militia during the War of 1812. Near the statue is a very old cannon, perhaps the same one that made him famous, or infamous, depending on how you read between the lines of history. At the foot of the statue is a bronze plaque describing the deed of heroism committed by O'Neil and his cannon.

In 1813 the British fleet entered Chesapeake Bay under the command of Admiral Cockburn. It anchored off shore.

As I read the plaque that summer of 1956 I learned that on May 13, 1813, O'Neil single handedly loaded the village cannon and fired on the British fleet. The recoil of the cannon wounded O'Neil. Understandably the Brits responded in kind, shelling the town. They then landed a sizable contingent of troops. The wounded O'Neil was captured and taken to the Admiral's ship, strangely named "The Maidstone." The Admiral intended to have O'Neil hanged.

Now John O'Neil had a beautiful daughter named Matilda and, according to the plaque, she bravely rowed herself to "The Maidstone" and begged to speak with Admiral Cockburn on her father's behalf. She was persuasive enough to have her father's life spared. The Admiral agreed to release him in return for the pleasure of burning the town to the ground. The plaque does not describe exactly what Matilda said or did which gave her plea such power of persuasion but the British commander did, indeed, release her father. The Brits returned O'Neil to shore, then put the torch to Havre de Grace and watched until it was a pile of ashes.

Some time thereafter the citizens of Havre de Grace determined that this man, who fired on an overwhelmingly powerful enemy fleet, suffered a self-inflicted wound, was captured then released in exchange for the total destruction of their personal and civic property, deserved to be honored with a statue. The chamber of commerce, or whoever writes their history, now claims that the British attacked Havre de Grace with 15 barges loaded with troops before John O'Neil fired at them in a heroic attempt to drive them off. Perhaps that is a more accurate account.

Some speculate the city fathers should have built a statue to honor the daughter who may have made a greater sacrifice for her fathers' life than he made for his town.

9. THE CHICKEN COOP

As we drove back out of town we passed a white, clap-board, single story building shaped like a long, narrow diner, the narrow end facing the street. Above it was a white sign with red letters that read "The Chicken Coop." A smaller sign below that boasted "Submarine Sandwiches, Soft Drinks."

"Sounds good," said Stan.

"Let's try it," said Bob.

"O.K." said I.

I pulled in and we climbed the three steps to the side door. Inside sat a pin ball machine, a juke box, three booths and a string of four stools along the counter. Behind the counter a short, 50ish year old, plump woman with a girlish face and ready smile was leaning forward on her crossed arms. She was wearing a white apron over her flower print dress. Her white hair was pulled back in a bun.

"Howdy," she said, while continuing to lean on the counter. "Jus' sit anywheres."

We sat at the counter and looked up at the printed menu hanging on the wall behind her. We ordered and waited while she fixed our submarines.

"Where y'all from?" she asked, "Bainbridge or Aberdeen?"

She had already deduced, despite our civilian clothes, that we were either sailors from the nearby Bainbridge Naval Training Center or soldiers from Aberdeen Proving Ground.

"We're at Aberdeen," Stan answered.

"Why do you call this place The Chicken Coop?" Bob asked.

Her pink, full cheeks framed a puckish smile as she replied, "'Cause that's what it is, or was. This whole thing, the diner part, the rooms in the back where we live and the two small rentals in the way-back used to be chicken coops. We began selling sandwiches when the military boys started coming around. When business got pretty good we pulled out the chickens, put in windows and doors, prettied it up and here we are!" she laughed.

While we ate several customers had come in, ordered takeout and left. They all called her Mom.

"Are they all your kids?" I asked.

"Naw," she laughed again. "Everybody calls me Mom. You can too, if you want."

So, we introduced ourselves and, as we left Mom called out, "Y'all come back now!"

I went there again, a few nights later. Mom was there with a man about 15 years her junior. With him were two children. She introduced him to me.

"This is Harry," she said. "My kids are all growed up so I got me another kid here to raise," she chuckled.

Harry was good looking with thick, curly red hair and one gold tooth at the front of his mouth that sparkled under the overhead lights when he grinned. He was also full of the devil, as I learned later. I assumed Harry was Mom's younger brother. He had two small children and never mentioned a wife. I later discovered that he and Mom were married and co-proprietors of The Chicken Coop. This was a second marriage for both.

A short time later a pretty young blonde girl of about 20 years wearing a white dress, stockings and shoes walked in from the door that led back to Mom and Harry's living quarters. Her outfit looked like a nurse's uniform.

"This is Jean," said Mom. "She lives in one of the back units and works for us nights and weekends. Jean, this here's Joe. He's from the Proving Grounds."

She took Mom's place behind the counter and Mom disappeared into the house. Harry sat next to me on a stool and the three of us visited between customers.

After a time Harry said, "Well, time for my show. Wyatt Earp comes on in a few minutes. You like westerns?"

I nodded yes.

"Well, c'mon back 'n join me," he said.

We went back to their living room. Harry turned on the TV, opened a couple beers and gave me one. Soon Mom joined us. Around 9 PM Jean closed the shop and joined us for a short time, then retired to her home in the back. The TV went off after the 11 O'clock news and I returned to the base.

And that started what soon became a routine. Several nights a week they invited me to come over to watch favorite shows on an old black and white TV. I was expected to appear without invitation every Tuesday night to watch Wyatt Earp. Jean usually worked the shop the last few hours, then joined us until the western was over. Occasionally I was invited to join them for dinner.

Joe and Joann Burns, a young couple, rented one of the units behind the Chicken Coop. They had been married four weeks when Joe, a sailor, was transferred to Bainbridge Naval Training Center to become a medical trainee. We developed a close friendship and I often visited with them. Between Mom, Harry, Jean, Joe and Joann I had found a family away from home.

As the Fourth of July weekend approached the town began to decorate the large park for a big celebration and fireworks. Tents went up, a bandstand was erected and vendors began stocking their wares. I was scheduled to march, in uniform, in the July 4th holiday parade through Havre de Grace. We made plans to get together after the parade. Mom and Harry were going to be working one of the tents that sold soda. Jean, Joe and Joann would be spectators at the parade and fireworks to follow.

On the night of July 3rd, while I was visiting in The Chicken Coop, Harry came in and asked if I had time to run an errand with him.

"Sure. What is it?"

"I gotta take the pickup and get some Coca Cola coolers for the soft drink tent. After Mom closes we'll go get it in Rising Sun."

Where's that?"

"Oh, not far," Harry answered.

I had discovered that Harry liked to drink. A lot. Hartford County was a dry county. You could drink to your heart's content inside a bar, club or restaurant but you could not, legally, buy a bottle to take out. Harry knew which house to go to, what door to knock on and what words to say to buy a bottle of anything you wanted. He also had an underdeveloped sense of responsibility. I had some reservations about this adventure but after he plied me with a couple bottles of beer I lost my apprehension.

After Mom closed for the night Harry and I got in his 1939 Chevy light pickup truck. He drove into town and stopped at one of the popular bars full of soldiers, sailors and tons of local gals. "We got time for one drink," he said.

The bar closed to outside customers at the legal closing time, but Harry knew the owner and his wife so the four of us stayed after closing time. Around 3:30 in the morning Harry, who had consumed considerable beer, stood up, stretched and, through a broad grin with a sparkling gold tooth said, "Let's us git goin! You drive."

He handed me the keys to the pickup truck and gave general directions to the small town of Rising Sun. He rattled off something that sounded like, "Take the main street back to the highway and head north. Then take MD155 to MD161 to US1, Conowridge Road goin' North-East then cross the Susquehanna over the old bridge and don't stop 'til you come to Rising Sun. Then wake me up." He promptly fell asleep.

I drove in a haze, trying to remember his directions, punching his shoulder to wake him now and then for specific directions but he soon didn't recognize anything. We got lost shortly after we crossed the river. We wandered narrow, two lane highways into what seemed to be open farm country. I began to think we'd never find it when we arrived at a small crossroads with a county sheriff's car parked with its headlights off. I pulled over and woke Harry. We got out and approached the sheriff car.

"Can we help you folks?" asked the Cecil County Deputy Sheriff behind the wheel.

"Sure can," said Harry. "Can you tell us how to find Holster's place in Rising Sun? We gotta pick up some soda pop coolers for the 4th of July thing in Havre de Grace."

"Well, now, whyn't you just follow us and we'll take you there," the deputy declared.

As we followed the deputy I said to Harry, "Man, when you leaned into that patrol car window I was dead sure that deputy would smell beer on your breath and lock you up for the night. All I could think of was how am I going to find my way back to Havre de Grace?"

"Aw, these guys know me from the Elks club. They wouldn't trouble me for havin' a drink. Anyways, you're driving, not me," he smirked.

Holster's place was a white, two story, barn-like house with a porch that ran clear around the front and both sides of the house. The deputies held a spotlight on the porch so we could find the steps and see several large Coca Cola coolers. As we picked the first one up and started down the stairs the porch light came on. A balding old man opened the door and stood there in his underwear.

"Hey, Harry," he croaked, "I was beginnin' to think you wasn't gonna get here."

"Just runnin' a little late," Harry said. "See you folks at the parade later on?"

"Yep. We'll be there." The door closed as we lifted the coolers into the back of the pickup.

The drive back took a while because Harry decided we should take a different route using small back roads to US 40 and over the big Susquehanna Bridge further south. This time we only got lost twice. We arrived at the Havre de Grace park around five thirty in the morning and carried the coolers over to some people who were setting up the soda pop stand. They took charge of the coolers so Harry and I could go home. Back at the Chicken Coop Harry asked me to come in for another beer but I begged off, reminding him that I had to get a couple hours sleep before the parade. I drove back to the base, and slept until noon.

Dressed in parade uniform I made it back to Havre de Grace just in time to join my platoon and march in the parade. Mom, Harry, Joe, Joann, Jean and several of her friends waved and cheered as we heroes marched by, straight backed, eyes fixed on the back of the guy in front, smartly in step. Twelve minutes of fame.

Following the parade I wandered back to join Joe and Joann in the park. We ate hot dogs, drank beer, visited with Harry and Mom, who were selling soft drinks out of the coolers, and listened to the music.

After dark we watched the fireworks, which lit up the sky. The flashes of light threw momentary long shadows of the memorial statue of John O'Neil whose lovely daughter, Matilda saved his life at the expense of Havre de Grace during the War of 1812— which some historians call "The Second War of Independence."

10. Apple On A String

Engineering and scientific text books, magazines and periodicals abounded in the S&P detachment. These were exceeded in quantity only by the number of science fiction publications to be found in wall and foot lockers. Science Fiction stories were often the subject of discussion, especially if the story bore some possible truth to it.

One such book was about a group of scientists who had determined that the earth was slowing in its speed of rotation around the sun. Their calculations indicated that when orbital speed dropped below critical speed the earth would tilt on its axis toward the sun, drawing closer until it finally collided with the sun, ending the earth as we know it. The scientist heroes of the book calculated exactly when this would occur. Their formulas and calculations were realistically presented in the text. They concluded that if they could detonate nuclear bombs at the North and South Poles, at just the right time, they could stop the tilt, maintain the earth's solar rotation speed and save the world. Of course, the book's heroes succeeded and the world lived happily ever after. This book was later made into a movie, but at this time it had just been published.

Two of our most avid Sci-Fi addicts were Walter Fish and Bruce Logan.

Walter spoke like a British citizen with a charming Cambridge English accent. He held a PhD in Mathematics, was an outstanding bridge player who entered master's competitions for fun, read mathematics text books for pleasure and was never "shaped up" enough to please our cadre. In January, 1959 Walt boasted to me, "The last time I shined this belt buckle was in July, 1956."

Bruce also held a Mathematics PhD. He was a balding young man, wore horn rimmed glasses and displayed a well rounded personality. He was, arguably, one of our most intelligent and admired people. His ready smile and witty humor contributed to his charisma. His opinion was respected. Everyone looked up to Bruce.

Coming across this book Walt and Bruce were intrigued by what they read in the Epilogue. Here the author confirmed his belief that the premise was real and the formulas were correct. His only concern, he wrote, was how to determine the exact moment when the earth's axis began its dangerous tilt so the atomic bombs could be set off at exactly the right time. He expressed the hope that someone in the scientific community would one day solve this problem.

The boys decided to have some fun with this author. They managed to get access to Post Headquarters letterhead stationery and typed a letter to the author. In it they expressed agreement with his premise, including bogus but authentic looking additional formulas and calculations of their own to confirm the author's conclusions. The letter went on to suggest that the exact moment when the earth's axis began to tilt could be determined by suspending a weighted ball on the end of a string. It included a Leonardo Da Vinci type hand sketch of the concept and explained that when the earth's axis began to tilt the ball would start to swing from the perpendicular. By watching this ball on a string the nuclear bombs could be set off at precisely the right moment. The letter concluded by thanking the author for his insightful work and implied that the scientists of Aberdeen Proving Grounds would pursue the concept and might contact him for further consultation when and if needed. They mailed the letter the next day.

The ball on a string solution was obviously simplistic. Even as its axis tilted the earth's own force of gravity would remain unchanged and would still draw the ball toward the center of the earth, just as it does now while the earth's axis wobbles through the four seasons.

The ball and string would probably appear to remain motionless to the naked eye unless the acceleration of the tilt was so severe as to be catastrophic. In that case, without sophisticated and complex computer technology to trigger the explosions, a visual observer would react too late. Further, the size of the bombs needed to stop such an event, and the resulting consequences would give pause to the most stalwart heart. It was clearly meant as a joke and the boys forgot about it after telling the story around the barracks for a few weeks.

The United States Postal Service was true to the famous quotation from Herodotus' Histories which is inscribed over the James Farley Post Office in New York City, to wit: "Neither snow nor rain nor heat nor gloom of night stay their couriers from the swift completion of their appointed rounds." The U.S.P.S. delivered the letter.

A week or two later Military Police at the main gate called General Holyfield's office. His secretary told the General that a published author was at the main gate. He had a letter, written on official Aberdeen Proving Ground Post Headquarters stationary, regarding a scheme to save the earth from falling into the sun. The author wished to offer his services as a consultant.

A huge furor resulted.

Many people were questioned to no avail. But it didn't take much detective work to match the typewriter that was used and check the date of the letter to the list of personnel who worked at Post Headquarters that day. They also reviewed which soldiers had pulled guard duty at the HQ building in recent weeks. Walter and Bruce were among those called in for questioning. Being honest to a fault they confessed. We saw neither hide nor hair of them for several days.

When the investigation was completed the boys were ordered to write letters of apology to the science fiction author. They apologized in person to General Holyfield. They lost all pass privileges for a while and were finally released back to the S&P Detachment.

Through the grapevine we learned when the boys were coming home. On that day a Military Police van was spotted coming down the road that skirted the quadrangle. Our spotters yelled out and the barracks emptied into the quadrangle field area. Over a hundred S&P troops crowded around the vehicle, applauding and cheering as it came to a stop.

The entire S&P Detachment stood in a large circle as Walter and Bruce stepped out, looking around and smiling. We parted, like the Red Sea, as they made their way toward the barrack. The crowd followed and watched noisily as they walked up the steps to the barrack door. Walt and Bruce swung open the door and froze, staring into the hallway then fell helplessly against the doorframe, laughing with the crowd.

A hanging bed sheet bore the message, "Welcome Home."

In front of it, suspended by a long string from the ceiling, was a large, red apple, swaying gently back and forth.

The earth was tilting.

II. ФТА

The letters FTA—an expletive that suggested an impossible sex act be performed on the Army—often appeared in various places throughout the base. As soldiers took small milk bottles from milk racks in the mess hall chow line the bottles deliberately left behind in the racks often, coincidentally spelled out the letters FTA. It was drawn on the rolled up mattresses left behind on empty bunks by GIs who had transferred out or been discharged, drawn on the dust on tanks and trucks parked in the motor pool lot and seen in the oddest places, much like the World War II "Kilroy Was Here" sketch drawn by American GIs all over the world. It served to vent the frustration of GIs and was instantly recognized by all who saw it. Officers of every rank, clear to the top, knew what it was when they saw it and knew exactly what it meant.

When General Holyfield, was about to retire a massive Retreat Ceremony was planned to be held on the parade grounds. All S&P soldiers were required to attend the retirement ceremony in full parade dress. They would be joined by another 500 troops from other organizations on base. The press would be there along with reporters for the army paper and several Washington DC, State and local officials. The base army band would play, awards and mementos would be given out and speeches of commendation and congratulations would fill the air.

General Holyfield didn't like the S&Ps. We didn't like him.

A scheme was hatched by a few of our more imaginative boys. They solicited donations and soon had $300. Armed with this kitty they set out for Baltimore to hire a skywriting service to print FTA in the sky over the city of Aberdeen during the Retreat Ceremony. Although the air space over the Proving Grounds was off limits to unauthorized flights the parade ground was well within sight of air space outside the base. As the day approached excitement grew. On the appointed day we learned that word had leaked to some of the officers in Headquarters. The officers appreciated how our detachment felt about the way Major Strange and General Holyfield treated "Joe Colleges" but also knew that heads would no doubt roll, and not necessarily those responsible. They had no desire to experience the wrath that was sure to come from the upper brass nor the media frenzy that would follow an investigation and possible prosecution of dozens of GIs. So, they decided to appeal to our two most distinguished members, Walter Fish and Bruce Logan of "apple on a string" fame.

The HQ officers met privately with Bruce and Walt and made a personal appeal, begging them to intercede to stop the plot.

On the appointed day close to 600 troops from various detachments and organizations stood in the hot sun, in full dress parade uniform, facing the raised platform decorated with the American flag, post colors and other paraphernalia. Most of the 130 S&Ps were there. All the dignitaries and brass showed up. The band began playing and speeches followed. As we sweltered in the heat many eyes scanned the skies looking and hoping. We did not know if the plot had been aborted or not.

The ritual droned on for what seemed like a couple hours but was probably much less. Near the end of the ceremonies General Holyfield stepped up to the microphone and began his farewell speech. His very young wife, a fine example of arm candy, looked on proudly.

Then it came, a small dot on the horizon, heading straight for us from the direction of Baltimore.

Someone whispered, "There it is!" Slowly all eyes turned up to the sky.

A soft murmur rippled through the ranks. The officers, sitting and standing on the stage, their backs to the city of Aberdeen, heard the murmur and noted our movements as 600 pairs of eyes raised upward to the sky behind the stage. Unable to resist, they slowly turned their heads to look up and over their shoulders. And there it was. They saw it, too. A single engine plane flew low over the town, just outside and parallel to the no fly zone of the base airspace. All held their breath.

General Holyfield, standing at the podium, engrossed in his speech, remained oblivious to what was going on above and behind him. He droned on, staring fixedly at his written speech. The plane banked toward us, then turned parallel to the edge of the forbidden air space and slowly began to waggle its wings. Six hundred faces smiled broadly and an audible titter rippled through the crowd as we recognized Ralph P., flying his rental airplane.

No FTA appeared in the sky but this was good enough for us. Every face, save Holyfield's, wore a grin. Every eye, save Holyfield's, was on our airplane as it looped twice around and repeated the waggle salute.

Ralph had, figuratively, put something nasty into the General's punch bowl at his farewell party.

12. Inspections

Periodic barrack inspections by the Inspector General (IG) were posted well ahead of time so troops could prepare by mopping, dusting, making beds and organizing window desks, wall and foot lockers in accordance with proper protocol. Bathrooms were scrubbed, the tops of window frames and wall lockers dusted, boots and brass shined. The IG's office usually sent a representative to conduct these inspections. Sometimes the Man himself came. Of course, they were preceded by inspections conducted by the Executive Officer and First Sergeant to prepare for the real thing.

During inspection each soldier stood at attention, next to his foot locker. The Executive Officer (EO), First Sergeant and one of his minions, accompanied the IG's representative as he walked from soldier to soldier. Uniforms, foot lockers, bunks, wall lockers, windows and desks were scrutinized. Soldiers were questioned regarding anything that appeared improper. Outright transgressions resulted in punishment, usually in the form of an Article 15, which could include extra duty and loss of privileges. The minion dutifully recorded each transgression on his clipboard.

The boys of the S&P Detachment were full of the wit and blundering which helped to make life at the labs and barracks bearable. Formal inspections sometimes provided just the right environment for creative mischief. For the most part inspections conducted in the S&P detachment went strictly according to Hoyle.

The troops generally met all requirements and the officers were happy. But there sometimes were exceptions. For example, the soldier who stuffed empty coke bottles into his display boots to keep them upright was restricted to the base for 14 days. Coke bottles inside boots were not in accordance with army regulations.

One of the more egregious pranks occurred when the IG, accompanied by some notables from Washington, visited the S&P detachment. After a cursory inspection of the barracks they retired to the Orderly Room. It was a hot summer day. The Orderly Room air conditioning system had been turned on as a special consideration for the visiting dignitaries. The air intake for the air conditioner was in the furnace room located at the far left end of the building. As soon as the inspection team and visitors returned to the Orderly Room and closed the door two men slipped out of second platoon barrack and into the furnace room where they had earlier stashed a supply of chemicals. When mixed and placed in front of the air intake the foul smelling gas they produced would enter the Orderly Room through the air conditioner vents. Rumors of the plan had been circulating beforehand so we watched from the windows. We saw the perpetrators enter the furnace room. We saw them leave. We waited. Nothing seemed to be happening.

Just as we concluded that the rumor was false the Orderly Room door flew open and there was a mass exodus of officers, visitors and cadre. With handkerchiefs over their noses and mouths they stepped out to the porch and down the stairs, waving hands through the air in front of their faces.

The detachment was placed on restriction for the weekend.

An area in each wall and foot locker is designated as "personal" and was the source of some mischief during inspections. Anything unusual, such as wooden blocks or a dried leaf, would be questioned by the inspection team. Typical justifications were, "Sentimental reasons, Sir" or "I think it is artistic, Sergeant"

Lowell Smith's bunk was next to mine. He was a sharp Nuclear Physicist who, in civilian life, owned Smith Research Laboratory in Lincoln, Nebraska. He designed and assembled electronic equipment as a hobby, sometimes mailing them to customers of his Nebraska laboratory. Lowell had assembled a black metal box with a small window on the front panel. Here the Greek letters ΦΤΑ—Phi Tau Alpha—flashed, in red, continuously. It was battery operated and completely sealed. The inspection team saw it sitting in Lowell's "Personal" space. The young IG representative, being new at this, simply stared with a slight frown. Lieutenant Timid, our EO at the time, suspected the English connotation represented by the Greek acronym but he wasn't about to open that can of worms. A worried look spread over his face. Sergeant Stephen was certain of its meaning but remained silent. In fact, unless the soldier admitted its intended meaning there was nothing he could do or wanted to do. There was no regulation against displaying three random letters of the alphabet, in any language.

Finally the IG could contain his curiosity no longer.

"What is that thing, soldier?"

Lowell stood at attention, staring straight forward, as he was supposed to do.

"An oscillator, Sir."

"What does it do?"

"It oscillates, Sir."

"What is it saying?"

"Phi Tau Alpha, Sir."

"Why?"

"Because that's what it's been designed to do, Sir"

"I mean what does that stand for?"

"The Greek letters Phi Tau Alpha, Sir."

"Why did you pick those letters?"

"It is a fraternal order, Sir."

"What else does it do?"

"Nothing else, Sir."

"Nothing else?!"

"No, Sir."

"Just blinks?"

"Just blinks, Sir."

He turned to his team, who deliberately avoided eye contact, and said, vacantly, "It just blinks. Huh. Weird!"

A couple bunks further along, on Bernie Hoefner's personal space the team noted two ball bearings sitting side by side. Nestled between the ball bearings stood a tall, narrow, rough surfaced rock with a knob shaped tip. At first glance it suggested a phallic display.

"Now what is that supposed to be, soldier?"

"Two ball bearings and a rock, Sir."

"Why in Sweet Jesus name would you have two ball bearings and a rock in your personal area!?"

"It is a metaphor, Sir!"

"A metaphor of what?" he asked suspiciously.

"It is a metaphor of contrasting forms of still life imitating real life, Sir!"

"What are you talking about, soldier?"

"Sir, the two ball bearings represent perfection in shape and symmetry. The irregular surface features and lack of symmetry of the taller rock represents erratic chaos, the polar opposite. The ball bearings support the bigger rock just as, in life, the sometimes more powerful but less cognizant are supported by the less powerful but more sophistic, Sir! "

The IG thought about this for awhile. He stared curiously for another moment. He turned to First Sergeant Stephen for guidance. The Sergeant, whom we had nicknamed Blinky because of the nervous eye twitch he had recently developed, looked helplessly at the IG with an expression that said, "Aw s--t, don't ask me!"

They continued down the aisle, approaching an empty bunk with rolled up mattress which had been vacated by Dave Scotto. Dave had been transferred to active reserve duty and returned to civilian life earlier this morning. This Jewish kid with an Italian name was a good friend. He had a deep sense of humor, good taste in dress and food and a level head most of the time. However, he was not above having fun at the expense of pretentious authority. Dave knew we were to have this inspection today. He also knew he would be well on his way home while we stood here at attention. He had deliberately left his wall locker closed. It was the only one on our floor with the door closed. It was not locked, just closed. It should have been left open.

We waited as the IG stopped before Dave's empty bunk and foot locker. Most IGs would have walked on to the next soldier. This IG was new, and young. He seemed perplexed, as if he had never before seen a closed locker during an inspection. He looked at Lt. Timid. Nothing. Again, he looked to Blinky for advice. But Blinky had been down this road before. His sad eyes implored the IG to skip it. He said nothing.

"Open it!" the IG instructed Blinky.

The Sergeant looked painfully into the IG's eyes, then to Lieutenant Timid for some sort of reprieve. Receiving none he walked reluctantly down the short aisle to the locker. He stood gingerly to one side as he lifted the tight latch that held the door shut. It seemed stuck and he had to lift it with both hands. Like a spring loaded mouse trap the locker door flew open, slapping Blinky's hands out of the way and clanging loudly against its hinges. A bald 710-15 auto tire, which had been compressed tightly into a tall oval, now released, flew out of the locker. It struck the empty army cot and flew upward, wobbling in the air, then it flipped onto the floor between the bunks where it spun madly. The empty cot and foot locker, bounced several feet into the aisle with such momentum they would surely have flattened someone in the inspection team had they not leapt aside; Lieutenant Timid to one side, the IG to the other, their dress caps twirling into the air.

It was a final farewell from David.

First Lieutenant Timid inspecting the latrines.

13. ARTICLE 15

I overslept one morning and had to rush outside for Reveille formation with less than five minutes to spare. When I got there I found that Blinky—First Sergeant Stephen—had blown his whistle five minutes early and started roll call. Apparently his wrist watch was running fast that day. He had already called my name and I had failed to respond. As I ran outside he stopped his roll call and began chewing me out for missing formation. Instead of keeping my mouth shut I pointed out, in what I thought was a respectful manner, that he had, indeed, begun roll call early. I was surprised by his angry response. Perhaps he felt I had embarrassed him in front of the troops.

Anyway, he gave me an Article 15 for being late to formation. It meant that for two weeks—Monday through Friday—I had to perform two hours of extra work after dinner (supper, for you Easterners). There was no set work assignment. The issuing officer could do so at his leisure. The usual punishment involved mowing the lawns, picking up trash and cigarette butts or doing drudgery cleaning of some sort. Sweeping, moping, waxing and buffing the floors in the Orderly Room was a very common Article 15 duty.

I served my two weeks of extra duty and on the following Saturday I drove to Havre de Grace and The Chicken Coop. Harry was there and was glad to see me again. Mom was busy making submarine sandwiches for a grey haired, distinguished looking gentleman sitting on a stool. His little daughter was sitting next to him. I took the stool on his other side and proceeded chatting with Mom and Harry.

Harry asked where I had been and I told him what had happened. I thought it would be humorous to share an exchange that had occurred between Sgt. Blinky and me one Wednesday morning in our Orderly Room. To make it humorous I exaggerated a little.

Blink: "Soldier, did you sweep, mop, wax and buff this floor last night?"

Me: "No, Sergeant."

Blink: "Why not!"

Me: "I didn't know what you wanted me to do last night. I tried to find you all day to ask but you weren't around."

Blink: "Wait a minute! You know damn well you're supposed to sweep, mop, wax and buff this floor every night! I told you that Monday night!"

Me: "No, Sergeant. You told me to sweep, mop, wax and buff this floor on Monday night but you didn't tell me to sweep, mop, wax and buff this floor on Tuesday night."

Blink: "Well, damn it! Aren't you smart enough to figure it out? Do I have to tell you every stupid little detail?"

Me: "Yes, Sergeant. *If I was smart I wouldn't be in this army.*"

Now, I didn't really say the last part but it made for a great story so I threw it in for Mom and Harry's amusement.

Blink: (biting down hard on his pipe) "Yeah!? Well, from now on if I don't tell ya ta sweep, mop, wax an' buff this floor, ya sweep, mop, wax an' buff this floor! Y'unnerstan'? I'm sick a' this bulls--t!"

As I finished talking, Mom and Harry laughed and the middle aged gentleman in civilian clothes turned away from his little daughter and looked at me with interest.

I figured he was probably a local business man or a high school teacher. The distinguished looking gentleman smiled and asked, "What company are you in?"

I was pleased that I had elicited laughter and interest from my audience and was feeling pretty cocky. Thinking I'd impress this civilian a little more I answered, "S&P Detachment, Ballistic Research Lab."

Then, to maximize his admiration I fabricated another exaggeration, "*We can get away with that sort of stuff more than most other troops on base.*"

Then I asked, smugly, "You ever hear of the S&Ps?"

"Oh, yes," he said as he stood up and turned to face me. "I happen to be the Battalion Commander of the First Battalion and just wondered if you were one of my boys."

He picked up his submarine sandwiches, turned smartly on his heel and walked out with his daughter.

I grew very small on my stool.

"THE BLINK"

First Sergeant Stephen; "Blinky."

14. Something for Nothing

Baltimore, Maryland lies about 30 miles southwest of Aberdeen. We had visited this colorful city many times. A favorite venue was a theatre that specialized in foreign films. It had stadium seating consisting of individual, stuffed, reclining, swivel seats. Wine, tea, coffee and demitasse were available for purchase in the lobby. We also visited downtown areas where strip shows and rescue mission homes are adjacent, vying to satisfy man at his extremes. We sometimes stopped in the strip joints for beer and snacks and to watch the strippers. The bar girls were aggressive. Most were hard as nails. One, to my surprise, was much too sensitive to be working in this environment.

She approached us, as they all did, and asked me to buy her a drink. I declined. A few minutes later she asked if I would like some company. I declined again.

When she approached a third time I said, "Look, I'm sorry, but I really didn't come in here for that." She recoiled as if I had slapped her.

Then, with a catch in her voice and a tear in her eye she answered angrily, "Well what did you come in here for, anyway!?" She stomped off into a back room behind a red velvet curtain and did not return.

The old red and yellow brick row houses, for which Baltimore is noted, were nearby. It was common, on sunny days, to see a housewife or two on each block scrubbing down the white marble steps leading up to the front doors.

On our way back to APG we often stopped at a diner called Molly's Place half way between Baltimore and Aberdeen. One evening Neil McKenna, Bob, Stan and I made the routine stop for coffee and something to eat. As we sat down to order Neil said, "Hey. See those two guys by the juke box? I know them from basic training." He got up, went over to them and brought them back to our table.

"Been to Baltimore?" one of them asked.

"Yep." Neil answered. "We went to the foreign film theatre to see 'Virgin Spring.' You?"

"We've been selling encyclopedias."

"Really?"

"Yeah. The money's pretty good. They trained us and it pays a 30 buck commission for each sale."

Well, that got our attention. We had been complaining earlier that we lacked money. Our monthly pay of $60 didn't go very far. One sale was half a month's pay. Neil asked for all the details and we eventually left with phone numbers and an address.

Neil did all the follow up calls. He and I made an appointment for an interview. A few evenings later we drove to Baltimore.

"Here it is, the Old Town Bank Building, 13628 Helena Avenue, Suite 316," Neil read off the map he had drawn. "Pull into the lot. They said they will validate the ticket."

We took an elevator to the third floor and found Suite 316. A small office held two desks just outside a glass enclosed conference room. A middle aged man in a business suit shook our hands and introduced himself as Samuel, our instructor and mentor.

"You're right on time." He walked us into the conference room where two others waited. After introductions and some small talk he began.

"Have any of you done door-to-door selling before?" No hands went up.

"That's good. It means we don't have to break any bad habits. We represent the Grolier Encyclopedia, one of the world's finest, price competitive encyclopedias. I'm going to show you a short movie that will give you an overview of the program. After that I'll give you some pointers. The whole thing will take about an hour. At 6PM the rest of the group will arrive and we'll go out and make some money. Let's get started."

The movie showed the encyclopedia set and the bookcase that came with it. Beautifully bound volumes stacked neatly on a bookcase that came in a choice of richly stained cherry or oak. The set came with a lifetime service that allowed the customer to write in for additional information on subjects included in the books. Once a month, for the next twelve months, the customer would receive an addendum volume with updated information. Then we saw a salesman knocking on a door and a woman answering. We watched the technique of the salesman, what he said and how he said it. The package cost a $30 down payment followed by twelve monthly payments of $24 for a total of $388. When the film was done Samuel turned off the projector and turned to us.

"I want to emphasis a few things that you just saw that are important to keep in mind." He went on to teach us a number of things, then gave us our new Grolier sales kits containing a large, fold-out full color brochure showing the product and a happy family, with smiling children. It showed several bookcases in two finishes, happy, intelligent young people doing well in school with open encyclopedia books in front of them.

At 6PM another 12 or so men showed up along with two more crew bosses. The next half hour was a question and answer period. Salesmen asked how they should have handled situations that had come up the previous evening. They were answered with advice and tips on how to overcome almost any objection a customer might come up with.

"Do you skip doors that have 'NO SOLICITOR' signs?"

"Never. People who put those signs up do so because they have no resistance to sales pitches. When you see one of those signs think to yourself, 'this one is an easy mark.' Ring that doorbell."

At 6:30 each crew boss took three or four salesmen with him. Each car drove to one of the hundreds of city blocks with large apartment buildings in Baltimore. Neil and I were dropped off, kit in hand, at different blocks and told to be back on the corner at 9PM sharp. I went from door to door knocking and trying to emulate what I had seen in the movie, to no avail. Afterward all the crew met at a small bar near the Grolier office. We bought beer and a split, fried hot dog on a roll and had our debriefing. Each salesman gave his report in three categories; entries, spreads and sales. If you made an entry it meant you got inside the apartment. If you managed to spread out your large foldout brochure and completed your sales pitch it was called a spread. And, of course, if you made a sale, well that's what it was called. So, each of us reported to the crew bosses by saying something like: "Six entries, four spreads, one sale." In my case it was "Five entries, two spreads, no sales."

Over the next few weeks Neil and I learned a lot about how to sell encyclopedias. For example:

1. Make sure both spouses are home before trying to make a spread so you don't waste valuable time only to be told, "I need to talk to my husband when he comes home. We'll call you." They never call you.

2. Remember, you are not selling anything. You are conducting a survey to find a qualified family to take part in an advertising campaign. Your company would like to place a free encyclopedia set with them if they qualify. All they need to do is tell friends about it and show it to their neighbors. Ask if they would like a free set of encyclopedia and for permission to come in to explain it.

3. Look at mailboxes for family names before you knock so you can embellish your introduction by saying convincing things like, "Good evening, Mr. and Mrs. Farmer. My company has selected you to receive a free set of Grolier Encyclopedia." They will be inclined to believe you since you already know their names.

4. Before leaving an apartment try to get leading information on the next one. "Do you know the family next door? What

is their name? Do they have any children? How many do they have? How old are they?" When you speak to the next family you can customize the pitch. "Research shows that most families acquire a good encyclopedia set before their oldest child is six (if their oldest child is close to six, for example.)"

5. Ask them questions that have obvious "Yes" answers. Get them used to saying "Yes." It puts the customer in a mindset of acceptance and agreement. "I know you want little Billy to get good grades in school, don't you?"

6. Never ask them if they want to buy the set. Never ask them to fill out or sign the contract.

7. Once you are well into the spread and have been getting smiles and yes answers move right ahead into their choice of the bookcase color. "Which color do you think would look best in this room? The cherry finish goes well with the drapes, don't you think, Mrs. Farmer?" Put a check mark in the appropriate box as soon as they agree on a color.

8. Start filling in their names while you talk. Avoid asking their permission to do so. Do not ask questions that could be answered with a "No." For example, as you are writing ask, "Is that F-A-R-M-E-R?" "Is this Unit 287?" They will be contributing to filling in the contract without being asked to do so.

9. When you have the contract filled in, slide right into the payments, but never use the word "Payments."
Say something like, "Now, if I gave you a free, brand new Cadillac you would be willing to put gas in it and keep it maintained, right?"
They will say "Yes." Smile and nod with a look that says, "Of course. Who wouldn't?" Then explain that you would like them to keep the encyclopedias current and in showcase condition for at least one year. To do this you will send them one updated addendum volume per month for one year. "All we ask is that you reimburse our cost of $24 per addendum."

10. At about this time many couples will express concern about the monthly expense. Tell them, "Actually, it amounts to about 79 cents a day - less than the cost of a pack of cigarettes and a cup of coffee."

    Remember, back then everyone smoked and drank coffee. They were probably smoking and drinking coffee with you as you spoke.

11. Now is the time to get a signature on the contract without asking for one. Here is how: while you are talking about cigarettes and coffee and gasoline, you will calmly, and without being noticed, fold the contract with a slight crease down the middle from top to bottom. Then, holding your pen at the top of the inside of the crease with your index finger, and using your thumb and middle finger as a back-up on the outside, reach the contract, bottom first, toward the one who seems to be in charge. It will usually be the husband. He/she will instinctively reach out to take it from the bottom. As he/she touches the paper, release the pen so it slides down the crease gently into the palm of his/her hand. We practiced this in the conference room until we got it right.

12. Once you have a signature on the contract you must get a $30 down payment. Do not use the words, "Down Payment." Use this: "We're almost done here. All I need now is $30 as a onetime token of your good faith." Then, shut up. Say nothing more. Don't be the first to blink.

I got pretty good at it and began making sales. My first was to a couple who could only raise $20. I knew I could accept less than $30 but it would come out of my commission. The instructors discouraged this. I was so desperate to make my first commission that I agreed to let them have it for a $20 token of good faith. My second and third sales brought in full commissions. Christmas was almost here and people didn't have extra cash. Selling became difficult. I did some calculations. I had earned $80 so far. But my half of the gas and the sandwiches and beer had cut into that. I also got a speeding ticket on Route 40 while driving to work. It cost me $11.45. I had just about broken even, so far. Neil was not doing much better and was thinking of quitting. I talked him into trying again after the first of the year.

The next time we went out I got lucky. The first door I knocked on was opened by a sweet old lady who told me she had no use for encyclopedias, but she suggested that Harold and Jean Walters, next door, had a two year old baby boy, Jimmy, and they might be interested. I rang the doorbell next door and was met by a young girl who explained she was the baby sitter.

"I'm here to see Mr. and Mrs. Walters. Are they home?"

She let me in. "They are just about to go out. You caught them just in time."

They came out dressed casually, each carrying a bowling ball case large enough to hold the ball and their bowling shoes. They were wearing matching team shirts.

I gave the opening spiel.

"Good evening. You must be Harold and Jean Walters. I'm not selling anything." They were hooked as soon as I greeted them by name and told them they had been selected to receive a free encyclopedia set as part of our advertising campaign. The hook was firmly set when I added that most successful American families acquired a good set of encyclopedia in their home by the time their first child was two years of age (like little Jimmy).

Harry looked at Jean and said, "Honey, we can be a little late for bowling. This is the chance of a lifetime. It's something that Jimmy should have. We've got to do this for him."

Of course, by the time baby Jimmy was old enough to read an encyclopedia this set would be a decade old and slightly obsolete.

When I got to the $24 to cover our cost for addendums Jean spoke up and said, "We don't have any extra money in our budget, Harry. Where will that come from?"

I talked about a pack of cigarettes and a cup of coffee and 79 cents.

"I'll cut down on my smoking," Harry said, smiling. "Instead of two packs a day I'll cut down to one and a half! I can do that."

"I don't need two big cups of coffee every morning," Jean said, brightly. "I'll use the smaller cups."

They did some math and concluded it still might not be enough. Harry looked at Jean and said, "Honey, if we skip bowling just one night a month we can easy come up with it. I want this for Jimmy. What do you say?"

She looked very serious, and then said, "OK. Sure. It's for him."

I was beginning to feel squeamish. This was surreal. In an almost hypnotic state I held out the contract. Harry held his hand out to receive it. The pen slide from my index finger, down the practiced crease, and into his open palm, like the serpent in the Garden of Eden slinking down the apple tree.

As he signed I explained about the $30 good faith money that I needed right then.

"Sure," Harry said.

He began to search through his pants pockets. Jean went into the bedroom and brought out a small purse. They scrounged until they had laid out what they had. Harry put aside ten dollars for bowling tonight and five dollars for the baby sitter. They counted what remained. Nine dollars and eleven cents.

"Honey," Jean said, softly. "If we stay home tonight we can use the bowling money and babysitter money. What do you think?"

The Babysitter, who had been listening, was caught up in the emotion of the moment and chimed in, "That's alright with me if you want to do that."

Harry counted it all again. Twenty four dollars and eleven cents.

"We're six dollars short. Six dollars!"

It grew quiet in the apartment. He stared at the floor. He looked up at his wife and with sorrow in his voice he said, "What'll we do?" He looked at me with pained eyes and ran his hand nervously through his hair. "This would be so great for Jimmy."

I felt terrible. These people had no business wasting their money on an encyclopedia set which would be of no use to them or their baby for years. I was tempted to tell them so but realized it would destroy their dream of doing something wonderful for the baby. I resolved to compromise and accept what they had on hand. Just as I opened my mouth to say so Jean jumped to her feet and said, "I'll bet old Mrs. Wilkins, next door, will loan us six dollars!" and she bolted to the door and down the hall. I struggled with a knot in my stomach. In a few minutes she came back, smiling and held six one dollar bills above her head triumphantly.

I closed the deal. They were so happy. I put everything back into my briefcase including the big colorful brochure and one signed contract. In my pocket was $30 worth of bowling money, babysitter money and one neighbor's loan. We said goodnight.

Harry and the babysitter walked to the elevator with me. He had to drive her home. I got off at the ground floor. Harry and the sitter continued on down to the parking garage.

Just before the elevator door closed Harry reached out to stop it and said to me with smiling eyes, "I was so scared. For the first time in my life I was getting something for nothing and I didn't have the down payment!"

I've thought about that statement many times since then. A down payment plus 24 monthly payments—something for nothing.

On the way back to Aberdeen I told Neil that I couldn't do this anymore.

He understood.

My encyclopedia salesman career was over.

15. Ruptured Retreat

Most S&P members drew guard duty at least once a month. The routine was to report at the guard barracks at 3 PM wearing a cleaned, pressed uniform with sparkling brass and shiny boots, ready for inspection. The Officer of the Day (OD) was a Lieutenant who had drawn that duty for the next 24 hours. He was in charge of the inspection, assignments of guard posts and overseeing the sounding of Retreat at sunset.

The OD selects the best dressed guard and that lucky guy gets to be the OD's driver. He does not have to stand guard at one of the posts. Instead he drives the OD around the posts once or twice during the long night.

He also drives the OD to the Post flagstaff in time for the "Retreat" ceremony at 5 PM. There they meet with a Flag Security detail which will lower and fold the flag. The driver will load and fire the cannon. He does this by putting a shotgun shell into a metal device which serves as a mini-breech with its own firing pin. The mini-breech and shotgun shell are then mounted and locked into the open end of an ancient cannon that sits near the flagstaff. He feeds the lanyard, which has a small weight on the end, down the cannon barrel until it comes out the open breech at the bottom of the cannon. The driver then takes his place at the cannon breech and holds the lanyard.

An unseen NCO, located in a broadcast booth inside the nearby Headquarters Building, plays recordings of the various bugle calls throughout the day. At 5 PM sharp this NCO starts playing Retreat over the base public address system. The OD's driver stands holding the lanyard, as the recording of Retreat is played. At the last note of Retreat the driver pulls the lanyard firing the shotgun shell with a loud blast that reverberates in the old cannon barrel and can be heard throughout the base. At the sound of the cannon blast the NCO in the broadcast booth starts playing the national anthem. The Flag Security detail lowers the flag in time with the music, completing the act as the music ends. All service personnel who are standing outdoors throughout the base stand at attention, facing the post flagstaff, holding a salute, until the national anthem ends.

That's how it is supposed to go.

Except for one time when friend Ralph P. won the honor for the first time. Ralph was a farm boy from the Midwest who had an advanced Electrical Engineering degree from one of the finest engineering schools in the country. He was a tall, slim, slightly balding, very likeable man whose love of aeronautics led him to take flying lessons every chance he got. Ralph was the hero of the General Holyfield retirement Retreat Ceremony when he flew a rented plane overhead, waggling his wings. He built his own working model airplanes and flew them on his days off.

On this day Ralph's spiffy appearance won the inspection competition. Although he disliked the regimentation and pomposity of peacetime army protocol he would gladly play the soldier game rather than stand guard duty all night. He grinned at us as he was selected and watched with delight as the rest of us were assigned to guard posts. We were each issued a carbine and one clip of 30 caliber bullets. This was the first time Ralph would rest while we stood four hour shifts all night long.

Later, as I was climbing into the back of the guard truck to be driven to my post Ralph walked by with the OD. They were leaving an hour early for the Retreat ceremony. Gloating as he walked past he grinned and said sotto voce, "Have fun out there you sorry bastards!!"

I arrived at Post #27, the motor pool, for the first four hours, or "first relief." A friend, Stan Wu, got off with me. He was assigned to Post #22, a large warehouse complex just across the street. After the truck left we walked to one of the many empty school buses parked nearby, climbed inside and broke out the submarine sandwiches we had hidden in our jackets. We listened for retreat as we ate.

"Can you picture Ralph standing at that cannon, all stiff and formal?" he asked.

"He's come a long way from the farm," I said, "and he sure enjoyed ribbing us about it, too!"

"Yeah. Just wait 'til we get back. He's gonna' tease us all night. Bastard!"

At 5 PM the music of Retreat played. We munched silently on our subs, safe inside our empty bus. As the last notes faded into silence we stopped chewing. No cannon shot. No national anthem. It was a full minute before we looked at each other. Another minute or so passed in silence, then the national anthem began without a cannon shot. In my head I heard the words to the anthem. A few lines into the melody, just as the song reached *"at the twilight's last gleaming..."* we heard the BOOOM!! Then the melody continued.

"Something went wrong!" I said.

"Yeah! Wonder what happened?"

Four hours later we went looking for Ralph at the guard barrack and found him lying on his bunk, his arms wrapped around behind his head, staring at the ceiling. We stood at the foot of his bunk and waited. Slowly his eyes drifted down from the ceiling and looked sheepishly at us.

"Well?" asked Stan.

"Wha' hoppen'?" said I.

"Aw, you wouldn't believe it," he whispered, and the story came out.

Ralph had shoved the shotgun shell into the mini-breech and fed the lanyard down the barrel to the rear cannon breech. He then seated the mini-breech in the mouth of the cannon. He took his place at the rear cannon breech and grabbed the lanyard with his left hand. Retreat played at 5 PM sharp. Ralph's sweating hand tightened around the lanyard as he faced the flagpole. The flag security detail stood at attention, flag halyards ready for the lowering of the flag. The Flag Security detail NCO stood at attention next to them, facing the flagstaff. At the instant the last note of Retreat faded the OD nodded and Ralph gave the lanyard a mighty yank.

What followed was not the powerful, echoing blast of a shotgun shell reverberating in the huge barrel of a defunct cannon but the metallic "tinkle, clank, tinkle, tinkle" of the steel mini-breech clattering down the length of the barrel. With a final clank it came to rest just below Ralph's clenched fist, the long, limp lanyard lying in loops at his feet. The mini-breech had not been seated properly in the mouth of the cannon.

The Flag Security detail stood rigid, holding the flag halyard, waiting for the national anthem to begin playing so they could lower the flag. However, the national anthem would not begin until the operator in Headquarters building heard the cannon blast. All around the base men stood at attention, facing the direction of the post flagstaff, awaiting the first notes of the anthem, half of them already holding a salute.

There followed a frantic attempt to extract the mini-breech from the rear cannon breech. Ralph had it out when the OD angrily pulled the mini-breech away from Ralph, ran to the mouth of the cannon and began to remount it himself.

"But Sir, the…"

"Get out of my damn way!" he said as he pushed Ralph aside. He dropped the lanyard in first, and then carefully seated the mini-breech in the mouth and properly locked it in place.

Ralph stepped forward again, "But, Sir the.."

"Move!" shouted the OD, pushing him aside again. The lieutenant grabbed the end of the lanyard and gave it a herculean jerk. Nothing happened. Consternation smeared across the OD's face. The Flag Security detail stared in horror at the OD.

"What the hell just happened!?" he shouted.

"The shell, Sir. It's here," Ralph said as he reached down between the OD's feet and picked it off the ground where it had fallen when the OD had jerked the mini-breech from Ralph's hands.

As Ralph recounted the story he added, "Well, the rest of it wasn't pretty. The OD kept dropping the shell as he tried to remount the damned thing. I never before heard that much foul language from such a clean cut young officer. He finally got it mounted. I was standing at the cannon breech holding the lanyard when he reached across in front of me, grabbed the lanyard and started to yank it."

Meanwhile, the NCO at headquarters concluded there would be no cannon fire and began the national anthem.

"Oh-oh say can you see, by the dawn's early light......"

The OD froze, the lanyard taut in his left fist. It was too late. He snapped to attention and saluted. The flag security detail began to lower the flag, with proper dignity. Their lead NCO saluted and cast a stern look at Ralph who was pinned between the cannon breech and the OD.

"What so proudly we hailed...."

Ralph saluted smartly. He flipped his arm up, finger tips touching his right eyebrow. His salute came up under the taught lanyard being held in the OD's fist and accidentally yanked it tight.

"At the twilights last gleaming..." "BOOOOM!!!"

"Well," Ralph sighed, "when we got back here the OD had to fill out a report for HQ. He pretty much blamed me, I guess."

Ralph never, ever again dressed up pretty for Guard Duty inspection. He decided being the OD's driver wasn't all it was cracked up to be.

16. Randy Bambi

There were countless stories associated with the experiences of the troops during guard duty. On cold winter days they sought refuge inside trucks or tanks to escape the elements. The motor pool garage, a large, barn-like building, was always warm and if one managed to be inside and out of sight when the civilian workers went home one would be locked inside the building. Two sliding bolts and an automatic, self locking bolt on a rear door could be opened from inside to let one out. With this access the guard could get out of the cold now and then.

It was rumored that one soldier arranged to be picked up by a friend shortly after being dropped off at his guard post. In the car he changed into civilian clothes. They drove off the base, attended a two hour movie in town, and drove back to the guard post. He changed back into military uniform and resumed his guard duties before the truck arrived with his relief. Most of us doubted this had really happened but it made a good story. An unconfirmed legend, as it were.

Aberdeen Proving Ground contained many wild deer. During rutting season one had to be careful not to walk carelessly into the path of a randy buck, as I did one night while on guard duty. I could hear the distant squeals of the bucks and an occasional clash of horns as I walked, in the moonlight, around a complex of empty warehouses.

Succumbing to the cold I entered one of the furnace rooms for warmth. I stared out of the small windows in the door, alert for the appearance of the Lieutenant who tried to make at least one round during the night. After a few minutes I put my warm leather gloves back on, slung my carbine and stepped outside. In the large, open space between myself and the next warehouse stood a tall pile of wooden pallets, stacked neatly in a pyramid shape. It wasn't until I had walked some fifty feet away from the building that I saw a large shadow moving around the corner of the far warehouse. I stopped and stared hard into the dark distance, trying to make out what it was. It moved toward me a couple steps and stopped again. I pulled the slung carbine off my shoulder and held it at port arms across my chest. This could be the Lieutenant. He would expect me to challenge him. The shadow moved again.

I shouted, "Halt!" as we had been taught.

The shadow stopped. I followed protocol and shouted, "Advance and be recognized!"

It stepped slowly forward toward me. After traveling almost half way to me I still could not tell who or what it was. I decided to stop him until I could make it out more clearly. I shouted, "Halt!" again.

This time it ignored me and continued to walk toward me. The protocol I was to follow was to lock and load one round of ball ammunition and shout, "Halt or I'll fire!" If the stranger then continued to advance I was supposed to remove the safety and fire one warning round over his head. Failure to stop after the warning shot gave me permission to shoot to kill.

I grabbed the bolt, pulled it back and slammed it home with a round in the chamber but before I could shout "Halt or I'll fire!" I realized I was staring at a large buck that was in cruise mode with a load of testosterone. It was suddenly clear to me that, in his eyes, I was just another randy competitor.

I gauged the distance to the door I had come out of and the pile of wooden pallets and decided I was closer to the pallets. As I broke into a run so did the buck. I reached the pallets and clambered up the pyramid. I heard clattering hooves strike the lower pallets. I kept climbing, tripping and stumbling, looking back after I reached the top. There he was, snorting and pawing, looking up at me, his front feet almost six feet above the pavement, leaning against the pallets. He was illuminated by a nearby security lamp. He was huge with an impressive rack.

We stared at each other for a while. He dropped to all four feet, snorted and pawed the blacktop. Then he stepped back and circled slowly, first in one direction, then the other, looking for a way to get up this strange hill. I wondered how long I would be stranded here. I considered shooting him, but dismissed the idea because it meant filling out reports. The ensuing investigation could turn out badly, especially if some officer decided I had not been chased and had shot the beast for the fun of it. I waited.

After some minutes he walked out of my sight into the darkness. I had no idea where he was now. He could be lurking nearby. He could be gone, chasing some doe after his successful defense of his turf. I remained standing on my wooden pyramid like a Robert E. Lee statue. It was almost an hour before I heard the sound of the 2½ ton guard truck coming to relieve me. As headlights lit up the area I clambered down and tried to look brave and confident. I whispered a warning to my relief guard, climbed into the back of the truck and contemplated how one of America's trained killers had been routed by a horny young buck.

17. Go Ahead, Make My Day

Early the next morning, sleepy, tired and cold, I again joined the others in the back of the truck. We were driven to the post stockade which housed other soldiers who were imprisoned for offenses ranging from simple Absent Without Leave (AWOL) to violent crimes.

As soon as we arrived we sat and listened to a lecture on our duties. The stockade Sergeant asked that anyone who had not received training with a shotgun should join him outside. I went outside every time so I could get to fire the weapon. About a hundred feet away was a high dirt embankment. On the plateau behind the embankment sat a large red barn. Before we fired at the embankment we were warned not to aim high and hit the barn. And, every time, one or two of the soldiers did shoot the barn. On this morning half a dozen workmen came running out of the barn, screaming foul language and shaking their fists at us.

After this instruction each guard received a shotgun with a full magazine of five shells. Each shell held five sticks of lead as big around as a short pencil. When fired, these five lead sticks splayed outward in a spinning motion. It was intended to kill whomever it struck, running through the victim like rotating scythes. At close range it would enter the body leaving an opening the size of a baseball and exit leaving a hole the size of a basketball.

Armed with this weapon we were assigned to guard prisoners during their work sessions that day. A work detail of two to four prisoners was assigned to each guard, depending on the task at hand.

There were two possible types of assignments. The least desirable one was to ride shotgun on one of the "white elephants." These were large, white garbage trucks with a steel tractor seat welded on top of the right, front fenders. Civilians drove the trucks throughout the base, stopping at each barrack to pick up garbage. Two prisoners sat inside the cab, next to the driver. The guard rode outside, sitting on the steel tractor seat, holding his shotgun, facing the cab front window so he could watch the prisoners. As the truck stopped, the guard climbed down first. Then he signaled the prisoners to come out of the cab and load the garbage. After each stop the prisoners got into the cab first. Then the guard climbed up to his steel fender seat. In winter the prisoners enjoyed the heated, comfortable cab while the guard suffered the purgatory of cold steel on his buttocks with wind and rain or snow on his back. In summer the heat and humidity enveloped the guard, his helmet liner acting as a plastic oven on his head while the prisoners sat in the shaded cab, the windows open to the breeze. The prisoners always found this amusing, grinning and making cat calls to the guard. The worse the weather the happier they were.

The slightly more desirable work details involved such things as moving furniture, or excavating dirt. In this instance the guard rode inside the back of a truck with the prisoners, sheltered from the elements, at least during the ride.

One of my more memorable assignments involved moving new furniture into several offices in the post headquarters building and removing the old furniture to a nearby warehouse. I was given four prisoners for the detail. We rode in the back of a 2½ ton truck with canvas roof and sides. The prisoners climbed up into the truck first. I ordered them to the far end against the back of the cab, then climbed up and signaled to the driver. He drove us to Headquarters building. The stockade Sergeant followed us in a military sedan. We got off in the reverse order; me first, then the prisoners. I walked behind them as the Sergeant led us into the building. Once inside he read from a work order and showed us which offices were to receive the new furniture. He instructed the prisoners on their work assignment. Then, he turned to me, handed me the work order and pointed to a phone number. He said, "That's my phone number. I'm going back to the stockade. If these bozos give you any trouble, call me."

After he drove off I stood in the office, my back to the doorway, shotgun in hand, watching the prisoners as they grudgingly began to remove the old furniture.

Slowly a pecking order appeared among them. The ring leader was a tall, muscular man with a nasty sneer and a pugnacious attitude. His buddy, a little shorter but equally tough, seconded every order the alpha male gave. The third, a heavy set hulk with a nasty scar on one cheek, quietly followed their orders and glowered at me through heavy eyebrows. Lowest on the totem pole was a chubby kid with pink, round cheeks who seemed flabby and slightly effeminate. He curried favor with the others by being the most vocal and defiant.

Suddenly one of them let out a wolf whistle and the smaller, chubby one chortled, "Oh baby! What a great pair of knockers!" I looked over my shoulder and saw one of the pretty young secretaries, blushing, walk rapidly down the hallway. I told them to knock it off. A few minutes later it happened again and the language was cruder. Again I warned them to watch their language and get back to work.

The alpha male sneered and said, "Whatta you gonna do, shoot us? Hell, there ain't nothin' you can do!"

Each time they saw a female employee the catcalls and abusive language increased. All four of them were hooting and making foul comments to the girls in nearby offices. No matter how threatening I became they ignored me and, in fact, became more defiant and belligerent. They were correct. I was helpless to stop their behavior. Even if they resorted to violence I could not fire a shotgun in this building full of civilians.

I picked up the nearest desk phone and called the stockade Sergeant. He said he'd be right there. As quickly as they had started the misbehavior they stopped. Fear crept over their faces. I told them to sit on the floor. They did. In a few minutes I heard the squeal of tires outside, the slam of a car door and stomping boots. In came the Sergeant.

"What's goin' on?!" he asked.

Where to start? I decided, like engineers do, to be methodical and organized. I intended to tell him what each had done, starting with the prisoner on my left and working my way across. The first on my left was the effeminate chubby guy. I pointed to him and repeated what he had said to the first secretary. Before I could say another word the Sergeant stepped forward, picked the kid up by his shirt front and slapped him hard across the face with a leather gloved hand. The kid fell backwards to the floor, blood running from his nose. The Sergeant kicked him twice, pulled him up and slapped him again, then threw him out into the hallway. He stormed out behind the crying, bleeding kid, kicking him in the buttocks whenever he caught up to him. As they reached the building exit the Sergeant called back over his shoulder, "Get your asses to work or I'll be back!" We watched through the windows as the kid was thrown into the back seat, which had no inside door handles, effectively locking him inside. The car spun wheels sending up a cloud of dust and pebbles, then hit the paved road with a screech of rubber.

For a few minutes the remaining three worked slowly and silently. Then the alpha prisoner started taunting me.

"Ya know what's gonna happen to the kid? Their gonna beat his ass and put him in the hole. He won't get nothing to eat today. All on accounta you, you son of a bitch!"

The taunting grew steadily worse, the language more vile. They finished moving in the new furniture and loaded the old stuff into the truck, talking trash all the while. As we rode toward the warehouse the threats grew in intensity and they took turns at it.

"Think you're f----n' tough! You're nothin' without that shotgun!"

"If you didn't have that f----n' shotgun I'd kick your ass you yellow, f----n' bastard!"

"First time you ain't lookin' we'll get ya! Gonna take that shotgun away from ya and stick it up your ass!"

"When I get out I'll find ya. Yer gonna eat s--t you bastard!"

"Look at him, he's shakin' in his shiny boots!"

My brain told me to ignore them, but a strange thing was happening. I felt guilty about what happened to the kid. I had not expected the Sergeant's violent reaction. I thought I'd be able to tell him what each of them had done, starting with the mildest and ending with the worst of them, the Alpha thug. I thought the Sergeant would chew them out, threaten them, and then leave. The kid was the least abusive of them and was clearly motivated by a need to impress his older, bigger cell mates. I should have done something different. My remorse turned to anger, at myself, at first, then at the sneering bullies in front of me.

About half way to the warehouse, with the load of old furniture, I did something that ranks among the most foolish things I have ever done. They had their backs against the back of the truck cab. I had my back to the open end of the truck. A wooden barrel stood about half way between me and the three of them.

"OK!" I shouted. "That's enough!!"

I pumped a shotgun shell into the chamber and took the safety off. They went silent and stared, bug-eyed. They backed flat against the cab's rear window, eyes fixed on me and the shotgun. I walked up to the wooden barrel and slammed the shotgun down on the barrel head.

"You think you're so damn tough? Let's find out! There's a shell in the chamber and the safety's off. I'm gonna step back from it. I'm gonna give you a--holes a chance to come and take the shotgun. Any time one of you big brave s--t heads is ready, go ahead! Make your move! Come and get it and shove it up my ass! But, when you move I'm gonna go for it, too."

They stared at me in disbelief as I took a step back, the shotgun lying on the barrel head. I stopped.

"Oh, one more thing," I said, holding up one finger. "You'd better reach it before me because if I get it first I'm gonna kill you with it! I swear to God! I get it first I'll blow a damn hole in you!"

Slowly I stepped back another couple yards until it sat roughly half way between us. My heart was in my mouth. I could hear my pulse throbbing in my temples. I saw their eyes flit to the gun, then back to me, then to the gun. I knew I had a slight advantage because the shotgun was positioned with the stock facing me. I could grab and use it without having to turn it around.

Still, what if they were faster than me? A minute went by, then another. Disturbing thoughts began to slither through my head. If I get there first will I really shoot? Will they? What will the authorities do to me when it is over, if I am still alive?

"Well?" I said, "Now's your chance to put your guts where your mouth is! Go for the damn gun!!" The adrenalin rush made it hard to keep my hands from shaking as they hung by my sides.

Another minute passed in silence as we stared, wild-eyed, at each other.

Finally, the number two guy, bouncing on his toes, turned to the leader and said, "Go get it! Kill him!"

Number three echoed, "Yeah! Go take it!"

The big bruiser looked at the shotgun, then up at me for a long moment. Our eyes locked. I could almost hear what he was thinking. He wanted to do it. There was a chance he could beat me. But then what? The army would hunt him down. Maybe they'd kill him. Or maybe he'd face a death penalty. Still, how could he back off after all the boasting and bragging? He had to try. He moved his feet apart and tensed as if he would spring forward.

His buddies immediately stepped away from him to the farthest corner of the truck. He noted their movement. Slowly, he straightened his posture, let his arms hang down again, turned his head to his admirers and said, "F--k you! You guys go for it!"

And it was over.

I walked up to the wooden barrel, picked up the shotgun and engaged the safety.

"That's what I thought," I said. "I don't want to hear another friggin' word from you the rest of the day! Not another damned word!"

The rest of the afternoon was quiet and uneventful.

That night, lying in my bunk I replayed what happened, over and over, thinking how incredibly lucky I was that something terrible had not happened. I had let my emotions overcome good common sense. I had needlessly put myself in harm's way to avenge a wounded ego and a feeling of guilt. It was stupid.

Still, I was pleased.

The cushiest guard duty assignment was to drive the 2½ ton guard truck. When I achieved enough seniority I applied for a truck class driver's license. They sent me to classes, then a test. Once I got that license guard duty got a lot better. Now I was the guy in the comfortable cab who the troops in the rear swore at as we went over railroad crossings and they bounced harshly on the hard, wooden benches. After each posting I returned to the guard house. Every four hours I got up from my cot or the TV room, drove the relief guards to their posts and picked up the old guards. Early the next morning I drove all of them to the stockade. I was then free to relax for the day until it was time to bring them back from the stockade.

I had a lot of time to read, sleep or visit, or wonder what had eventually happened to that chubby, rosy cheeked young prisoner.

18. Sputnik

Although it was not generally broadcast to the public at the time we, at the US Army's Aberdeen Proving Ground, were keenly aware that a significant part of the cold war with the Soviet Union was the race to conquer space. An artificial satellite would offer many military advantages, including the ability to spy on enemy activity from space. The CIA and President Eisenhower were already aware that the Soviet Union was preparing such a program. The United States Army Ballistic Missile Agency (ABMA) had proposed a program called Explorer which would use the Army's Redstone Rocket technology. This technology, which was successfully developed to deliver intercontinental ballistic missiles to an enemy, had the capability to launch the world's first orbiting satellite. The Explorer program was stalled when the government asked for proposals from all three services. The Air Force, Army and Navy then submitted individual proposals. Washington awarded the program to the Naval Research Laboratory (NRL) and labeled it Project Vanguard.

A major consideration in making this decision was that the Navy proposal used rockets that sounded like civilian products rather than military missiles, which were thought to be inappropriate for peaceful scientific exploration. What went unstated at the time was that the U.S. already had a covert satellite program underway, WS-117, which was developing the ability to launch spy satellites using USAF Thor IRBMs. The US government was concerned that the Soviets would object to military satellites overflying the Soviet Union. The idea was that if a clearly "civilian" and "scientific" satellite went up first, the Soviets might not object, and thus the precedent would be established that space was outside any national boundaries.

The Soviet Union, however, had no such qualms. On October 4, 1957, they used one of their R7 ICBM rockets—a powerful military rocket—to launch Sputnik into orbit. This 23 inch diameter satellite weighed 183 pounds, circled the earth once every 96 minutes and emitted the first man generated sound from space—a steady "beep – beep – beep." The world was astounded.

As I arrived at the lab that morning Tom, Art and Ony were excitedly talking about the news broadcast that announced the Soviet achievement. Tom and Ony were heading out the door.

"Where you going?" I asked.

"To the mothball fleet to get a radio," Tom said.

They left with a tool box and drove out to an airport area on base that housed, among other things, a fleet of retired World War II bombers. There they pulled a radio from one of the bombers and within a couple hours they had connected it to a roof antenna and set it to the frequency the Soviets had announced. We held our breath as the static cleared and a small, steady beep came clearly over the speaker. It gave us goose bumps. Our cold war adversaries had beaten us into space. Other members of the staff came to our small cell to hear the radio and discuss, in passionate, sometimes heated terms, the frustration of knowing that the United States had the capability to enter space for some time and was losing that race for political reasons.

I was scheduled to pull Kitchen Police duty the next day. My routine for KP was to set an alarm for 2:45 AM, get to the rear porch of the mess hall before other soldiers and be first in line so I had first choice of duties when the cooks arrived to unlock the mess hall door. I would select the garbage detail, which was the most desirable job. I'd have little to do until after each meal. The guys who cleaned up the mess hall brought the garbage cans out to the area where I worked. My job was to make sure they were properly filled and the area was hosed down and clean after each meal. However, during and between meals I could flatten and spread out a clean cardboard box and catch up on my sleep. Later in the day a truck showed up to pick up the garbage. I believe pig farmers bought this garbage to be used as feed. Once they left I hosed out all garbage cans and the surrounding area with scalding hot water. The cook would do a quick inspection and I was free to leave.

On this morning, however, I did not curl up on the porch floor to await the cooks. Sputnik was scheduled to appear as a bright speck in the sky at 3:35 AM. So, with a line of other soldiers gathering behind me I studied the star studded sky. Suddenly it appeared just above the horizon of trees. My fellow soldier-engineer-scientists let out an audible sound of wonder as Sputnik, gleaming with ghostly reflected light from the hidden sun crawled across the sky. It resembled all the other stars in that Maryland sky except that it was moving. I imagine no one of us will ever forget the feeling of seeing, for the first time, an object made by man, sailing overhead in earth orbit. And the men who did so were Russians. And, on that magic morning, we scientists and engineers were standing in line to perform KP duties for the rest of Aberdeen Proving Ground.

It was disheartening.

The Vanguard Program sputtered frustratingly. Launches, when they finally happened, resulted in embarrassing failures.

On November 3, 1957 the USSR launched Sputnik II.

On December 6, 1957 the United States attempted to launch Vanguard TV3. The rocket rose about four feet into the air when the engine lost thrust. The rocket immediately sank back down to the launch pad and exploded. The payload nosecone detached and landed free of the exploding rocket, the small satellite's radio beacon still beeping.

On the night of January 31, 1958 the US Army launched the first United States satellite, Explorer I, using technology from the Army's Redstone family of rockets, the family we had wanted to use before Sputnik I.

Finally, on March 17, 1958, the Vanguard I satellite was launched and achieved orbit. It was 6 inches in diameter, was solar powered and weighed 3 pounds. Soviet Premier Nikita Khrushchev dubbed it "The Grapefruit Satellite."

The mighty United States had been embarrassed by the Soviet Union. Concern with the sorry state of our vaunted technological superiority swept the nation. Money became available to encourage engineering and scientific careers and programs.

Yet here, at Aberdeen Proving Grounds, for the past half dozen years, a detachment averaging 130 soldiers, many with advanced degrees in engineering and scientific fields, were being used to guard prisoners and empty warehouses and to perform mess hall duties. Word reached some of our congressmen. Articles appeared in the Baltimore Evening Sun, one of the largest East coast newspapers.

On November 29, 1957 the following article appeared:

"Misuse At Aberdeen Charged" "Experts Doing K.P.?"

"The Army is 'grossly misusing' 130 scientists at Maryland's Aberdeen Proving Ground by putting them on KP duty, a Congressman charged today.

Representative Albert W. Cretella, Connecticut Republican, charged the Army exempts less important personnel from routine duty, while keeping expert technicians on it.

He specifically singled out the Army's scientific and professional program, which is designed to utilize talents of trained enlisted men.

'It should be re-evaluated or completely scrapped,' he said. 'Gross mis-utilization of these persons. . . . appears to be the rule rather than the exception.'

At Aberdeen, he said, two thirds of all enlisted men are exempt from KP duty. This group includes military police, bandsmen, instructors, clerks, firemen and the entire medical detachment.

Not exempt are the 130 scientific and professional personnel, he declared.

Cretella remarked, sarcastically: 'It is enlightening to know that in the American Armed Forces, a filing clerk or a tuba player is more indispensible to the needs of the Army than a mathematician who is doing research on ballistics.'

Morale of the enlisted scientists at Aberdeen is 'shattered' he charged. Their incentives are 'stifled,' he added, and quoted an unnamed chemist as saying:

'They know no fear because Russia sent a rocket 900 miles into the atmosphere, but mention that a general is coming to inspect their shoe shines and fear grips them.'"

On November 30, 1957 a follow-up article quoted the Congressman as saying that a physics professor had quit his civilian job at Aberdeen because of **"disgust with the inefficiency and incompetence of the proving ground."** The professor said four soldiers who had worked under him on the scientific program spent about half their time **on 'KP, guard duty and the like.'**

In a following article the paper reported, *"The commanding general of the proving ground admitted here today that scientific and professional specialists are being used part-time on KP, but added that there was nothing he could do about it.*

Maj. Gen. Carrol H. Deitrick, post commander, said the Army's regulations require that scientific and professional men serving in the Army be given the same details that any other enlisted man is given, with no exceptions. His hands were tied, he averred.

Baltimore radio station WBAL, boasting 50kW, the highest signal strength in the area, began broadcasting anonymous interviews with soldiers who were assigned to work in the Research laboratories of Aberdeen Proving Ground but were spending most of their time performing mundane tasks such as KP and guard duty for the thousands of other troops on the base.

Reporters were contacting individual soldiers and conducting interviews in a beautiful yellow Corvette whose back seat area and trunk were loaded with recording equipment. They clandestinely met at a bar in the next county, dressed in civilian clothes. In the bar the reporter urged each to make notes in preparation for the interview. They then retired, one at a time, to the Corvette for a recording session.

The radio station began a series called, "The Voice of Science." It broadcast every half hour for several minutes. After an introductory statement they played an interview with one of the soldiers, and then they concluded with, "You have just heard the voice of Science."

Our Executive Officer, First Lieutenant Timid, quizzed a number of us several times and paced his Orderly Room nervously as the broadcasts continued relentlessly. His concern was primarily that this would reflect badly on his personnel file if he were held responsible.

First Lieutenant Timid hears the "Voice of Science" broadcasts on Baltimore Radio station WBAL.

Newspaper articles and radio broadcasts blanketed the Washington DC area. Congressmen began asking questions. Proposals were introduced to change the program so these engineers and scientists could do full time research at the laboratories. Some congressmen began to lobby for an early release program so we could return to the civilian work force. The military launched an investigation aimed at finding and punishing the soldiers who were giving interviews to the papers and radio stations.

All of us were questioned at one time or another. Those who had taken part in the interviews were able to recognize their own voices on the radio and read their own words in the newspaper. The military investigation was not able to identify any of the participants. The media protected their sources.

The Army issued a bulletin to all personnel entitled, "RELEASE OF INFORMATION." It read, ***"Department of the Army recently announced changes pertaining to the release of information to the public. It is important that APG personnel, including USAOTC, familiarize themselves with Sec 42, Vol 1, APG Procedure Manual. It is necessary that any information released to non-military groups by speaking engagements or writing articles be cleared in advance by the Information Office, Hq, APG. (ORDBG-IO)"***

It was an exciting time.

Eventually the Army changed the active duty draft obligation of critical skills engineers and scientists from 24 months, down to 21 months, 18 months, 6 months and eventually did away with the active duty obligation. However, none of us already in the service under any of the old programs were allowed to leave early. We were made to complete the full term. We gave two years of our lives on active duty and 4 more in reserve status but were not recognized as military veterans. We received no military benefits, no life insurance, no reduced interest home loans, no educational assistance and no VA medical benefits. We were the lost veterans.

When I completed my two years of Active Duty and was transferred to Active Reserve, later that year, the S&P program remained unchanged.

Military tradition prevailed over enlightenment.

"Traditions are like lampposts. The wise use them to light their way, drunkards to support their instability......"
Count Leo Tolstoy—a Russian.

19. Farewell To Arms

Every single man in the S&P Detachment could tell you, on any given day, exactly how many months, weeks and days remained of his mandatory two years of active duty. As a soldier's time grew short he developed his own way of reminding his buddies. We classified ourselves into two categories; long timers and short timers. Anyone with less time than you was a short timer. Short timers walked around saying such things as:

"Geez, ya know, I've got less months left than you have years."

"I've got less weeks left than you have months!"

"I've got less days left than you have weeks!"

And, in the last hours of that final day, "I've got less hours left than you have days!!"

And so it went.

The mandatory draft occasioned by the Korean War had ended a long time ago. New arrivals consisted of volunteers who were assigned elsewhere. There were very few college graduates coming along who had received deferments during the war. As our short timers were transferred to Ready Reserve the ranks of the S&P Detachment shrank.

We went through several Executive Officers in the S&P Detachment during those two years. At first they were, like us, engineers and scientists who had received deferments and were now serving their mandatory time as officers. As they transferred out to other assignments or to discharge they were replaced by Regular Army officers, volunteers who chose a military career. There was a notable change in attitudes and behavior.

Captain Bowman was our first EO and was one of our most popular officers. On his last day he called us out on the quadrangle and gave a short speech. His last words, delivered with a smile were, "Gentlemen, it has been a challenge."

He was followed by Lieutenant Ebber, another EO we considered "cool." Highly intelligent and eminently fair he was too good to last. Shortly after his arrival he was discharged. During his short stay he made many friends and we put on a grand retirement party for him.

A quartet sang "Take down your service flag, Mrs. Ebber, your son is now an old S&P!" to the tune of My Bonnie Lies Over The Ocean.

This was followed by a chalkboard presentation, done as a mathematical proof, which developed the expression:

Tolerability = Remaining Time + Soul's Resurrection Upon Discharge - Damage Done × Grey Hairs Since Induction ÷ Fudge Factor To Replace Logic As Seen Fit

This was expressed by symbols denoting variables. Then it was simplified by substitution of terms, which was too lengthy to reproduce here, and reduced to:

$$\text{(Typical U.S. Attitude)} (1/A) \div F = T$$
$$\text{And thus: Typical U.S. Attitude} = FTA$$

As a finale Lieutenant Ebber was presented with a scroll designed by one of our guys with the inscription Illigitimus Non Carborundum, or loosely translated, "Don't Let The Bastards Wear You Down" which, we explained, made him an honorary member of our enlisted men's Greek fraternity ΦΤΑ!

Lieutenant Ebber was replaced by Lieutenant Timid, who we nicknamed 'Timmie.' He was often referred to as "Jack Armstrong" and "The God Child" because he was always so Bristol neat, and proper. His demeanor was formal and distant in a rigid, unfriendly way.   Lt. Timid was with us for a long time before he shipped out. On his last day he, too, gave us a short farewell speech while standing on the Orderly Room porch.

"I was forewarned about you guys when Duty Sergeant Child greeted me on my first day. He said, 'These guys are different.' He was sure right!"

Lt. Timid was replaced by Lieutenant Pain, a pompous, dictatorial persona who became one of our least appreciated EO's. This man, with a southern drawl that seemed deliberately exaggerated, enjoyed mispronouncing names as a sign of his contempt and superiority. He played harassment games with soldiers he didn't like by rejecting three day weekend pass requests for arbitrary reasons.

"I want your name typed all in capital letters."

Then, the next time, "I want your name in lower case with just the first letter capitalized."

He made a practice of informing soldiers of his reason for rejection just minutes before he left the base for the weekend. Thus the soldiers didn't have a chance to retype and resubmit the request. Lieutenant Pain would walk out to his car and drive off, smiling, while the soldier was still typing an arbitrary correction.

After a while we learned all the petty reasons for his rejections. We made a practice of preparing and submitting half a dozen requests at one time, each corrected for a past rejection. He had to sign one of them as it was against Army Regulations to refuse a weekend pass without legitimate cause.

One day Lieutenant Pain ordered us to stand outside the orderly room for an announcement. He stood on the small porch, looking down at us, stiff and pompous, like Hitler at the parade grounds in Nuremberg. He told us that Major Strange had asked all Executive Officers to strive for a 100% participation in donations for the upcoming Joint Charities Appeal. He made a speech about the importance of contributing. He said he expected 100% participation. Then he made a major error. He ended his talk with a threat.

"Anyone who doesn't contribute to this charity will never get another weekend pass! You will rot on this base!"

Lieutenant Paine got his 100% but in reverse. Not a single S&P donated to the collection point in the Orderly Room. Every soldier was called in and threatened. Every one of them reported he had already donated at the Joint Charities Appeal office in the city of Aberdeen and produced a receipt. The boys of S&P knew their Army Regulations. It was illegal to extort money from soldiers. Lieutenant Pain had earned the distinction of being the only Executive Officer on base to reach a zero donation percentage. When he was transferred out of Aberdeen Proving Grounds Lieutenant Pain gave no farewell speech. He simply left.

I began losing close friends whose active duty time was up.

One of our very favorite and most colorful S&P soldiers was Nick Eliopolous whose ancestors had emigrated from Greece to Philadelphia. He had a delightfully dry sense of humor and a wry wit. Nick was short of stature with an Abraham Lincoln sort of plainness. His thick, black hair, bristling eyebrows, dark, deep-set eyes, undershot lower jaw and permanent 5 o'clock shadow gave him a menacing look. His arms and legs were disproportionate to his body. His short torso, very long arms and short, bowed legs defied the army uniform to look normal. It always seemed ill fitting.

Nick had taken four years of Reserve Officers Candidate School while in college and passed all the tests with flying colors. He was planning a military career. With his stellar college grades he had no reason to doubt he would serve his military obligation as an officer. Instead, on the eve of graduation he was flunked out of ROTC for "A Lack of Military Bearing." In other words, he just didn't look like what they thought an officer should look like. He was hurt and very bitter toward the military establishment.

Nick spoke in a slow, precise manner. His intelligence and humor were second only to his creativity and imagination. He built the "Grecian Lamp" out of an old, empty, Greek wine bottle. It was grotesque but the inspecting officers did not force him to remove it from his bunk area because he was allowed to have an "artistic" decoration in his designated personal space.

Nick sketched excellent caricatures of our Executive Officers. His drawings became popular collector's items with the troops.

He created a mythical "Murder Incorporated" with Friday Night Specials and for comic authenticity he carried a cheap metal cap gun loaded with strips of real caps. He called it "my rod." When targets of opportunity appeared outside the bus that carried us to and from the labs, Nick carefully slipped the cap gun from inside his jacket, aimed and "eliminated" the unfortunate officer with a loud bang!

On December 19, 1957, he was discharged. I drove him to the bus terminal and waited with him in the rain. We sat in the car and shared memories. As the bus pulled up he turned to me and gave me his "rod."

His parting words were, "I've had it for several years but it isn't of sentimental value. I've killed no dignitaries with it, only little shits like Pain, Timid and Strange. You keep it."

I laughed and shook my head, looking at the cap gun in my hand, so tiny, ridiculous and symbolic.

"Remember," he said, referring to the whole Army experience, "it's only a game. You have to play it with them."

His face was serious and thoughtful – then he shook my hand and smiled.

"Good luck, Joe. Thanks for the ride and Merry Christmas."

He was gone in the rain.

I spent more time with Bernie Hoefner after that. This mathematician was an aspiring playwright, sensitive, short, and a little on the plump side. He was a gifted wordsmith and composed profound letters to Senator Javits in the United States Congress, pleading the cause of the misused and abused S&P troops. As a consequence he endured unusual harassment from our EO, Lt. Timid and base officers, Major Strange and a mysterious Colonel Clutch none of us had ever heard of before. Colonel Clutch appeared out of nowhere and his sole purpose seemed to be to harangue and annoy any troops who had complained to congressmen.

Bernie's sharp sense of humor kept my remaining days illuminated with bright moments. One day, as we sat looking out the windows at the rain Bernie said to me, "When Nick Eliopolous left one of the last great army legends left. There are only two legends left now, you and me."

A few months later I drove Bernie to the bus station. With one foot on the bus step he looked back at me, grinned and said, "Look for me on Broadway. One of these days they will marquee my work!" Then he was gone.

As my time drew near I made the rounds of the laboratory and barracks to say goodbye. I drove one final time to Havre de Grace to bid farewell to Mom, Harry, Jean, Joe and Joann at the Chicken Coop. It was a bitter-sweet feeling. I looked forward to returning to civilian life, the old friends and familiar places. Yet, this was a place full of many pleasant memories. I was at once exuberant and melancholy.

As I collected my things and drove away from the quadrangle I couldn't help but look back, now and then.

I showed the MPs at the gate my papers and was waved through. I turned right on Highway 40 and passed the turn-off to Havre de Grace, drove over the bridge above the Susquehanna River where its mouth emptied into Chesapeake Bay and stepped hard on the accelerator.

I was going home.

Going home.

Epilogue

When I reached Philadelphia along Route 40, I stopped to visit Nick Eliopolous. He took me to the art museum which was designed to imitate the Parthenon in Greece. We ate lunch and reminisced one last time. Years later I wrote to him at his retirement home in Florida and mentioned I no longer had the cap gun. He wrote back that if I was after his remaining pearl handled one I could not have it.

Bernie Hoefner has no doubt made the big time on Broadway. I think he changed his name for marketing purposes, so I scan every new stage hit and try to guess which one was written by Bernie.

I was on a business trip some twenty years later that took me close to Aberdeen Proving Grounds. I rented a car and drove through town. Nothing seemed familiar. I could not find the diners I frequented, the movie house, the drive-in or the Happy Clam. I saw no USO.

I drove to Havre De Grace. The Chicken Coop was gone. No one in the neighborhood remembered it. After some detective work I found a neighbor who had a phone number for Jean. I spoke to her on the phone. She was married and had three children. She told me Mom had died some years ago. Harry died soon afterward. He went out drinking one lonely winter night and did not come home. They found him in a snow bank the next day.

I drove to the city park on the edge of Chesapeake Bay. There was the statue of John O'Neil, hero of the War of 1812, next to his old cannon. He did not remember me.

∞

After leaving Aberdeen Proving Ground I went on to serve three more years of active reserve and one more of standby reserve in accordance with the old six year enlistment program.

But that, as they say, is another story for another time.

HISTORICAL NOTES

The space race continued with the Soviet Union landing the first man made item, Luna 2, on the surface of the moon on September 13, 1959. In 1961 President John F. Kennedy announced our intention to overtake the Soviet Union in the space race and land men on the moon by the end of the decade. United States astronauts, Neil Armstrong, "Buzz" Aldrin and Michael Collins orbited the moon with Apollo 11 on July 20, 1969. The following day Armstrong and Aldrin became the first two men to walk on the moon.

The cold war between the Soviet Union and the United States continued for another two decades. Eventually the Soviet government weakened and the union began to dissolve. During the period from January 19, 1990 to December 31, 1991 the USSR republics declared their independence, effectively ending the cold war.

Currently 18 European countries plus the USA, Canada, Japan and Russia are cooperating in the construction and operation of the International Space Station whose mission is to develop and test technology for spacecraft exploration systems and to support potential future missions to the moon and Mars. To date the station, which flies in low earth orbit, has been visited by astronauts and cosmonauts from 15 different countries.

∞

On May 31, 2011 the following appeared on the official website of the United States Army, WWW.ARMY.MIL:

APG leadership briefs Congressional staffers.
May 31, 2011

ABERDEEN PROVING GROUND, Md. -- The installation is quickly becoming the U.S. Army's hub for science and technology, APG senior commander Maj. Gen. Nick Justice told staff from Maryland's Congressional delegation March 30.

"This place will be the biggest success story in BRAC," Justice said, referencing Base Realignment and Closure that is bringing thousands of high-tech jobs to northeast Maryland.

Representatives of U.S. Sens. Barbara Mikulski and Benjamin Cardin and U.S. Reps. C.A. Dutch Ruppersberger, Andy Harris and Roscoe Bartlett gathered at the Berger Laboratory Complex at the start of their APG tour.

Because of BRAC, APG serves as the headquarters for several of the Army's science-focused commands, including U.S. Army Test and Evaluation Command; U.S. Army Research, Development and Engineering Command; and Communications-Electronics Command.

Justice also discussed another installation priority -- to build, renovate and demolish. He said World War I barracks are still standing on the Edgewood Area.

"We've torn down 54 buildings this year," Justice said. "It takes an incredible effort to decontaminate the materials in those buildings.

"We're looking to get those torn down because they cost us money. They're wasteful, and they're not good for our environment."

About The Author

The author served six years as a member of the United States Army during the uneasy armistice following the Korean War. The first two years were on active duty stationed at Aberdeen Proving Ground where he worked on military research and development programs. He was there when the Soviet Union successfully launched Sputnik and brought sudden urgency to the United States space program as an important weapon of the Cold War. Like other soldiers of that time and place he was affected by the conflicting agendas of the scientific community and military establishment and determined to memorialize that unique period.

Joseph Manfredo is also the author of *Only The Living; a memoir* and *After Midnight; poems and pontifications.* He is retired and living in Southern California.